Heal Your Memories
Heal Your Life

Master Your SOUL Lessons

SIRSHREE

Heal Your Memories, Heal Your Life

Master Your Soul Lessons

By **Sirshree** Tejparkhi

Copyright © Tejgyan Global Foundation
All Rights Reserved 2022

Tejgyan Global Foundation is a charitable organization with its headquarters in Pune, India.

ISBN : 978-93-90607-19-8

Published by WOW Publishings Pvt. Ltd., India
First Edition published in July 2022
First reprint in December 2022

Printed and bound by Trinity Academy, Pune, INDIA

Copyright and publishing rights are vested exclusively with WOW Publishings Pvt. Ltd. This book is sold subject to the condition that it shall not by way of trade or otherwise, be lent, resold, hired out, or otherwise circulated without the publisher's prior written consent in any form of binding or cover other than that in which it is published and without a similar condition including this condition being imposed on the subsequent purchaser and without limiting the rights under copyright reserved above, no part of this publication may be reproduced, stored in or introduced into a retrieval system, or transmitted, in any form, or by any means, electronic, mechanical, photocopying, recording or otherwise, without the prior written permission of both the copyright owner and the above-mentioned publisher of this book. Any person who does any unauthorized act in relation to this publication may be liable to criminal prosecution and civil claims for damages.

Although the author and publisher have made every effort to ensure accuracy of content in this book, they hereby disclaim any liability to any party for any loss, damage, or disruption caused by errors or

To
Saint Kabir
who conveyed the profound truth
of the urgency to heal the human fabric,
to be returned in the same pristine state
as bestowed upon us.

Contents

	Preface	7
PART 1 - THE LEARNING SYSTEM IN EARTH-LIFE		**11**
1.	Cleansing The Soiled Body-Mind Fabric	13
2.	The SOUL Purpose	19
3.	Who Really Is Living My Life	24
4.	Understanding Karmic Bondage	28
5.	The Pillars of Karmic Bondage	32
6.	Karmic Bondage Due to Injured Memories	38
7.	The Memories-to-Lessons Connection	43
PART 2 - MANIFESTATION AND HEALING OF INJURED MEMORIES		**49**
8.	The Self's Script for Healing and Growth	51
9.	The Play of Memories – 1	57
10.	The Play of Memories – 2	62
11.	The Play of Memories – 3	66
12.	We All Have Been Chosen	70
13.	Confronting Karmic Scars	75
14.	The Tools for Healing – 1	80

15.	The Tools for Healing – 2	86
	PART 3 - THE LEARNING APPROACH	**91**
16.	The Benchmark for A Successful Life	93
17.	The Urgency to Learn Our Lessons	98
18.	Heeding The Voice of Conscience	107
19.	Recognizing Your SOUL Lessons	112
20.	The Learning Mindset	117
	PART 4 - A DEEP DIVE INTO OUR SOUL LESSONS	**125**
21.	The Lesson of Patience	127
22.	The Lesson of Unconditional Love	134
23.	The Lesson of Courage	142
24.	The Lesson of Persistence	148
25.	The Lesson of Empathy	154
26.	Other SOUL Lessons – 1	158
27.	Other SOUL Lessons – 2	164
28.	Other SOUL Lessons – 3	170
29.	The Final Lesson	180
30.	Our Impersonal Mission	185
	SOUL Lessons and Their Contributing Challenges	189
	Appendices	193

Preface

Life on Earth
An Invaluable Opportunity

Hundred gods were graced with the opportunity to descend upon Earth for a brief period of life. They had to choose between two kinds of physical forms to be born with. The first form was susceptible to various feelings, while the other was incapable of experiencing any feelings.

But there was a catch. The first form was vulnerable to intense feelings. While they could experience joy and elation, they would also be subject to uncomfortable and painful emotions, troublesome moods, and a depressed state of mind. It was a more complex and challenging choice. But there was a positive angle to it. Accepting this form would open the possibility of uncovering an invaluable treasure hidden within them. They would attain supreme bliss and lasting freedom after discovering the treasure.

However, if they chose the second form, they would neither face any complex feelings nor know about the treasure, let alone uncover it.

The gods were presented with these choices. It turned out that fifty gods chose to be born with a form devoid of emotions so that they could enjoy life on Earth. As a result, they also accepted the impossibility of finding the treasure. They were born into the plant and animal kingdoms. Devoid of complex feelings, they led a mundane existence.

The other fifty gods were prepared to take up this challenge and live against all odds considering the possibility of uncovering the treasure. They chose the form that was capable of feeling deep emotions. They were born as human beings!

This mythical story carries deep hints for us. The first hint is that beyond our earthly form, we all are an expression of God. Every wave that rises in the ocean seems to have a separate existence. Yet, it is an integral part of the ocean. When the wave crashes, it merges back in the ocean. Similarly, our earthly existence is an integral part of God, and our bodies are vehicles for experiencing and expressing divinity.

The second hint is actually a good news. We chose to be born as human beings, for which we should congratulate ourselves. The human form is far more complex than plants or animals but can uncover the ultimate treasure hidden within us. Our feelings and thoughts may cause suffering but understanding them opens the way to unravel the treasure.

The beauty of Earth-life is its magnificent learning system for which our body-mind mechanism is primed. Whether we know it or not, this learning system is constantly at work in every aspect of our life. In schools and universities, we first learn our lessons and are then tested. But in the school of Earth-life, we are tested first and then learn our lessons!

Earth-life is a marvelous teacher that imparts lessons to us through testing situations. It constantly throws circumstances at us until we learn the lessons they were seeding.

SOUL lessons are the key lessons of life that enable us to realize our innate potential. They help us discover and develop the latent qualities seeded within us. To discover and appreciate something positive, we need to contrast it against something that *seems* negative. The value of courage is realized in the face of fear, love in the face of hatred. Just as the seeds of higher qualities are implanted within us, so are the seeds of painful feelings.

You would have heard the proverb: There is no gain without pain. In the context of the priceless opportunity of human life, this proverb should rather be re-phrased as, "There is no gain without *understanding* pain." In this context, "gain" is the treasure of bliss and freedom.

But confronting sorrow is often uncomfortable for many of us. How can understanding our painful feelings lead us to such a treasure? How can we follow the very causes of sorrow to get rid of them?

Consider how a detective works. With a magnifying glass in his hands, he looks for clues, and once he finds them, he pursues them until he reaches the root of the matter. We, too, as self-detectives, should follow our painful thoughts and feelings with the magnifying glass of awareness until we learn our SOUL lessons.

This book explains how we can heal painful memories that have a burdening influence on us. It unravels the deepest mysteries of the divine design of life. Equipped with this understanding, we can fulfill the real purpose of our life on Earth.

The book has four parts.

Part 1 – The Learning System in Earth-life: It explains the design of human life that facilitates learning and evolution. It explores the reasons why we experience challenges and conflict. It throws light on the four invisible factors that burden and constrain us.

Part 2 – Manifestation and Healing of Injured Memories: This part elaborates on the karmic bonds that infest our memories.

Replete with stories of healing of past life trauma, this part describes the wonderful arrangement of nature designed for us to learn our SOUL lessons. It explains how to cope with the fallout of our painful memories and provides tools for getting rid of karmic bondage.

Part 3 – The Learning Approach: It discusses the prerequisites for learning our SOUL lessons. It establishes the urgency of learning, the mindset required for it, and the ways to recognize and learn our lessons.

Part 4 – A Deep Dive into Our SOUL Lessons: This part delves into the key SOUL lessons that are part of the curriculum for most of us. It then touches on other lessons that pertain to dealing with relationships and achieving inner growth.

We have been trying to solve life's problems and are often perplexed. But this book opens the possibility of not just dissolving these problems but going beyond to the state of indescribable bliss.

You would have played the board game of snakes and ladders, where the ladders propel you up, and the snakes pull you down. Life, too, is like a game of snakes and ladders! What if you realize that the problems you are entangled in are the ladders that take you to your highest joy and greatest freedom?

This book explains the art of *converting* snakes into ladders in the game of life. It sheds light on what's holding you back from achieving true progress and lasting contentment. It empowers you to tide through life's challenges fearlessly.

So, without further ado, let us begin to understand the learning system of life on Earth.

PART 1

THE LEARNING SYSTEM IN EARTH-LIFE

1

Cleansing The Soiled Body-Mind Fabric

On his visit to a nearby town, a man borrowed his friend's shawl to protect himself from the severe cold. He wore it not only during the day but also for sleeping at night. The shawl got creased and soiled. Now, he wouldn't return the shawl in such a condition.

So, the following day, he washed, ironed, and prepared it to be returned. The friend was supposed to come in the evening to take the shawl back, but he didn't. So, this man got to keep the shawl and use it that night. On the third morning, he again became ready with a washed and pressed shawl for his friend. But his friend didn't turn up yet again. The man was gifted one more day to use the shawl.

When this went on for a few days, the man settled into using the shawl and stopped bothering about washing or pressing it. Gradually, he forgot that he had to return it to the friend!

So it is with human life. We are not human beings choosing to undertake a spiritual journey. Instead, we are spiritual beings who have chosen to embark on this human journey on our visit to Earth. We are gifted with the intricate fabric of the human body-mind for this Earth-life. We get to wear this wondrous fabric until it is taken away. More importantly, this human fabric ought to be cleansed and ironed out to remove the inner creases that develop during worldly life so that it can be returned in its pristine form, just as we had received it.

Saint Kabir's couplet beautifully conveys this -

Chadariyaa jheeni re jheeni
Ram naam ras bheeni chadariyaa
Panch tattva Gun teeni
Thok thok ke beeni
Chadariyaa odh sankaa mat kariyo
Ye do din tum ko deeni
Murakh log bhed nahi jaane
Din din maili keeni chadariyaa
Das Kabir jatan se odhi
Jyon ki tyon dhari deeni chadariya

***

This fine garment, woven with great care,
Dipped in the essence of the Lord's name.
The fiber of five elements and the pattern of three gunas,

> *Pressed together in a tight weave.*
> *While wearing this garment, have no doubt,*
> *It's loaned to you for only two days.*
> *But the foolish don't understand this,*
> *And keep soiling it day by day.*
> *Kabir Das wears it with such care,*
> *Hands it back just as it was gifted to him.*

The fabric of the human body-mind is the most wondrous creation. The Creator has rendered it with great care, pouring immense joy and purity into its design. The human body-mind comprises two layers – the gross physical body and the subtle mental body.

Consider a motorcycle fitted with an outer car body. When you ride the motorcycle, it would appear to onlookers that you are driving the car. Similarly, we may outwardly perceive that the physical body is interacting with the world. But the physical body is only an Earthly vehicle for the expression of the mental body.

When we ride the motorcycle with the car body around it, does it mean that we are the motorcycle or the car? No, we are neither. Drawing parallels, we can conclude that we are neither the subtle nor the gross body. Who-we-truly-are is beyond both body and mind. We get to use the body and mind during the life on Earth.

It is indeed a grace that we get to use this body-mind every day from morning till night. Life can be a song of gratitude that venerates this grace. But when we do not recognize this opportunity, we get caught up in the bitter experiences of daily life. We lead a mechanical existence without awareness, responding to circumstances in the same old programmed ways and living the same old days repeatedly. It rarely strikes us that we have received this body-mind on loan to return in the same pure form we had received.

Let us not fritter away the very purpose of why we are here on Earth. Life on Earth is a short visit. When we see someone ninety years old, we may feel he has been here for a long time. But time is an illusion. We cannot measure the duration of our Earthly visit by clocks and calendars, but by how much we have learned from our life experiences. Since we are not clear about the purpose of this short visit, we keep contaminating our body-mind. Before we even realize it, it's time to return.

The human garment becomes stained and dirty when subjected to sour and bitter experiences of worldly life. The experiences we gather while going through everyday situations, dealing with people, get imprinted on the mind and pollute it. We feel frustrated when things don't work as we'd like. We become resentful and angry when people scorn or reject us. When situations appear gloomy or hostile, lethargy, despair, and hopelessness take over us. We feel unstable or indecisive in the face of challenges. All these feelings leave deep impressions on our psyche, polluting our mind. These impressions can be called karmic scars, which cause bondage. We will understand more about karmic bondage in the further chapters.

Out of ignorance and lack of awareness, the gross body accumulates karmic scars. These scars, in turn, get etched on the subtle body, forming tendencies. If these scars are not erased, they are carried forward with the subtle body into the life after the death of the gross body.

Let us understand how these karmic scars are etched with the help of an analogy. Whenever you write on the top page of a notepad, your writing pattern gets etched on the page below. The second page will show you the impressions of your writing. This is called a subtle pattern. Similarly, whatever you write on your gross body affects your subtle body.

How do we know that our soul fabric is polluted? As such impressions accumulate over the years, we begin to sense an unknown burden and incompleteness while moving through the tides of life. Despite enjoying comforts and a solid financial backup, we may still feel an emptiness, a restlessness, as if something is wrong. We yearn for inner peace and contentment. All these are symptoms of a stained mind.

A lotus grows in muddy waters and yet remains pure and clean. Just as the lotus flower remains untouched by the mud, Kabir remained untouched by the allure and illusion of worldly life. He was immersed in devotion. Only those, who live like a lotus, can return their soul fabric in the same state as it was received. To live the life of a lotus means to fulfill the whole and sole purpose of Earth-life while maintaining a spotless soul fabric.

If one doesn't recognize the mud, then in all probability, he will get mud stains on his dress. A blind man can get stained with mud. Similarly, our soul fabric will get stained if we lack awareness or understanding of how our thoughts, feelings, speech, and actions cause karmic scars. But once we imbibe the understanding provided in this book, we will develop the eye of wisdom that will help us cleanse and safeguard our soul fabric.

Saint Kabir's handing back the fabric to God exactly as it was gifted to him means that he didn't let any stain sully his soul fabric. How many of us can proclaim, "When it was time, I could return my soul fabric in the spotless state as it was bestowed to me. I could save it from all stains."

A pregnant woman is very careful about her baby. She walks cautiously, taking care that the baby in her womb is not subject to any trouble. She is aware that her eating, sitting, standing, walking, or sleeping in the wrong way could harm her baby. Each of her deeds is carefully measured. She does all this because she loves her baby. It is love that awakens awareness, tenacity, and patience.

We, too, need to elevate our awareness and develop urgency to erase the stains that are formed on our subtle body. When we live with this conviction and use every situation in our daily life as an opportunity to work on our inner purification, we live an awakened life. Instead of becoming victims of circumstances, we consciously choose to convert the snakes in our life into ladders for growth. Then challenges become springboards to elevate us.

In and through our daily activities, we should remain vigilant that our body-mind shouldn't get stained by our thoughts, feelings, speech, or actions. Such vigilance is a prerequisite for living a fulfilled life.

When we lead such an awakened life, we fulfill the purpose of our human incarnation – the SOUL purpose. For this, we need to develop certain vital qualities that take us to the pinnacle of human evolution, where we become one with the Creator. We need to learn certain key lessons, which can be called SOUL lessons.

What is the SOUL purpose? What are these lessons? We will discuss this in the next chapter.

2

The SOUL Purpose

Once upon a time, a wise, generous man lived in a village. He had a son who loved him dearly.

The noble man wished to know about the neighboring city by getting some first-hand experiences, but he couldn't go there himself. Those who returned from the city gave an intense and vivid narrative of their experiences.

His son was eager to fulfill his father's wish. Mustering all the courage, he offered to visit the city to learn about life there and bring back some invaluable experiences for his father. The wise man was overjoyed by his son's courage and resolve and blessed him as he embarked on his mission.

The son arrived in the city late at night and settled in a lodging, excited about what was in store for him the next day. The next morning, the son was jolted out of sleep by the heat in the room and some voices shouting around him, "Fire… fire…." He sprang out of his bed and rushed to extinguish the fire by calling the fire brigade. He lost half of his day in this process and the rest in fatigue and frustration. He couldn't venture out to the city as planned. "Never mind," he said, "I'll go sightseeing tomorrow."

The next day, the same episode repeated. His house caught fire, and he frantically ran about resolving the issue. When the same episode repeated every day, he was annoyed, "Who is setting the house on fire every day? I can't find time to visit different places in the city I've heard of."

He started looking around for the culprit. He suspected his neighbors, room service, and many others he encountered around his house during the day.

When a month passed by, he was dejected at his plight. He rarely got the opportunity to visit the city and shoot video clips and pictures of its beautiful vistas. He spent most of his time in firefighting.

Frustrated and desperate, he decided to focus his efforts on finding the root cause of the daily fire. Imagine his rage and disbelief when he discovered that his father was setting his house on fire every day. He couldn't understand why his father would do this to him. Enraged, he started cursing his father, for whom he had embarked on this mission to the city.

Finally, he communicated with his father and lamented in anguish, "Why did you do this to me? Why did you send me here only to make life so difficult? I thought you wanted me to visit and learn about the beauty of this place. But you've made it so painful for me here!"

The father smiled lovingly and said, "My dear child, I love you deeply and unconditionally. Life back in our village is jolly and peaceful. However, it doesn't offer you an opportunity to grow. We grow only in the face of challenges. City life isn't just about the rosy side you were looking forward to. All that is rosy and beautiful only helps you sustain yourself. But the unexpected, demanding, and intimidating situations bring out the best in you. You woke up every morning to a fire, but this fire was meant to awaken you to your pristine nature!

"Life in the city is a contrast between ups and downs, joy and sorrow, good and bad, love and hate, anger and peace. There is so much richness and vastness in the range of experiences that this contrast offers you. When you lack a higher perspective of life, you keep blaming people and cursing situations. When you gain that higher perspective, you see opportunities in the face of challenges. Enrich yourself from the experiences you gain. That's what I want you to learn and bring when you return to the village."

This story bears a resemblance to life on Earth. Indeed, life on Earth is much like life in the city that overwhelmed the young man. We are here on a short visit to gather certain experiences that can help us discover our pristine nature. Our true nature is unconditional love, lasting happiness, untouched peace, boundless compassion, infallible faith, and endless creativity.

Earth-life offers us the opportunity to uncover two qualities hidden within us – unconditional love and unshakable faith. The discovery and expression of these qualities can be called our SOUL purpose. That's why we have incarnated at this time in this social setting. Our SOUL purpose is the whole and sole purpose of our life. Earning a livelihood, raising a family, building a career – whatever we do in life is an inherent part of our SOUL purpose.

SOUL is an acronym that can be expanded as **S**teadfast **O**bedient **U**ntainted **L**oving. Thus, our SOUL purpose of Earth-life is to develop a steadfast, obedient, untainted, and loving mind.

Steadfastness

Our mind tends to waver in situations. It shakes when faced with challenges. We are swept away by emotions like fear, despair, anger, and resentment. Our self-belief and confidence quiver when threatened by people or circumstances. Our focus and resolve can deviate from our goal. We get deluded by scenes that don't seem like what we want them to.

Steadfastness is a key quality of the mind that we need to develop. The mind should be unshakable, resolute, and persistent to not deviate from our goal.

Obedient

We express ourselves through our thoughts, feelings, speech, and actions. Too often, we find that what we think is not what we speak, what we feel is not what we do, and what we do is not what we say. When our expression in life becomes fragmented, we lack integrity, and our vitality gets depleted. Life becomes complicated and scattered.

An obedient mind has the core quality of integrity, which is essential to achieve lasting success. All our energies are focused when our thoughts, feelings, speech, and actions align in one direction. Life becomes simple and powerful.

Untainted

We had a pure, fresh, and innocent outlook as a child. But, as we moved beyond the age of two, we start getting conditioned by our parents, neighbors, teachers, peers, and off-late the social media. When the mind is subjected to a storm of events in daily life, it gathers negative impressions. These impressions shape its perspective, distorting the way it sees the world.

The mind needs to be purified by eradicating the filth of tendencies and impressions. The tendency to react in fixed patterns leads to a mechanical way of living with lowered awareness. Such tendencies and impressions need to be brought to light through the power of daily introspection. An untainted mind serves as a clean mirror to reflect our true self.

Loving

The ego begins to form when we move beyond the age of two. The ego is the feeling of being separate from everything else. As a result, our underlying oneness is lost, leading to feelings like insecurity, self-centeredness, hate, and malice.

All such negative feelings dissolve with the remembrance of our essential oneness and realization of our true nature as the Universal Self. One of the key aspects of the SOUL purpose is to sublimate the ego in devotion, leading to the experience of unconditional love. Such a loving mind naturally exudes compassion and forgiveness.

These vital qualities cannot be developed in a classroom or coaching session. Our daily life is the classroom, and events and situations are part of the curriculam that helps us nurture these qualities.

3

Who Really Is Living My Life

We are not just thinking machines; rather, the thinking machine is an instrument that we use. Careful observation will reveal that we are not our bodies since we can observe our bodies as an assembly of parts. Whatever can be observed cannot be the observer. Even our thoughts can be observed. We can take some time out to observe our thoughts as they arise and subside. With practice, we find that we are not our thoughts. We are the knower of our thoughts, the knower of our mind. This knowing continues even in the gap between thoughts.

This knowing or Consciousness is the essence of life. It is the Source of life from where everything arises. It is who-we-truly-are, beyond our body and mind. Consciousness is experienced as the feeling of beingness, being awake to whatever is happening. This song of beingness is being played constantly; we are that song. Being aware of this song gives the experience of pure joy, unconditional and boundless, independent of the world, untouched by situations.

Our Beingness is the source of creation, the wellspring of inspiration. When we don't tap into this, our thoughts are limited by what we see in the world.

When we connect with this inherent joy, inspired action arises automatically. We need to inculcate the practice of frequently dipping into the stillness of Consciousness. This enables us to bring our Beingness into our actions. Our thoughts and actions are then imbued with freshness, delight, and creativity.

The Universal Self – beyond the individual

Consider a machine that comprises several parts. Every part of the machine, whether small or large, whether it plays a major or a trivial role, is merely its part. The parts do not function individually for themselves. Rather, the machine functions *through* them.

What if the parts of the machine were to believe that they were working for themselves? What if they believed in existence independent from the machine? Wouldn't they be blinded by such a limited view?

You see the machine working as one whole. The parts are merely instrumental for the larger purpose of the machine. The story of the parts is a partial reality. The purpose of the machine is the complete reality.

In the same way, due to a limited view and ignorance of the complete reality, we believe that *we* are leading an independent and individual life. The truth is that the Universal Self or Consciousness is living this story we call as "my life." When we consider ourselves as individuals, separate from the Universal Self, we remain oblivious to the purpose of the whole.

Consider a sheet of paper on which words are written. The paper exists behind the words and also between them. The words cannot exist without the paper.

Drawing parallels to human life, we see numerous individual life forms, but the background of all these, the Self, is one. The Self is the source of all manifestation. It permeates and enlivens our physical and mental existence. Individual human life is merely a part of the expression of the whole on the screen of consciousness.

The human body is non-living. It springs to life in the presence of consciousness. Knowing happens through the medium of the body and mind. Thus, it is not the body or mind that knows. It is consciousness that knows and expresses through the medium of the body-mind.

Imagine a painter who paints a picture of a paintbrush. This paintbrush comes to life and serves to create more paintings for the painter. However, if the paintbrush assumes its own individual existence and a separate personal purpose, it will go about painting without consulting the painter. Though it was created to explore and manifest the painter's creative inspiration, the paintbrush will do everything else without fulfilling the painter's original wish.

In the same way, the human body-mind mechanism is the manifestation of the Self. It serves as an instrument or a medium to manifest the Self's further creations. But due to the shroud of illusion inherent in Earth-life, we live as separate individuals instead of allowing the Self to experience and express its Oneness. Though individual and group creations do happen in the visible realm, they are largely devoid of true and lasting contentment.

Karmic bondage – the contamination of pure consciousness

Suppose you write on a sheet of paper. What happens when a carbon paper is placed beneath this sheet? Impressions are formed on the other white sheet of paper below it.

Here, the carbon paper represents the collective mind of humanity. Whatever thoughts or emotions we entertain cause impressions to be transferred through the universal mind (the carbon paper) and etched on pure consciousness (the white sheet of paper below it).

When we assume ourselves to be the individual body-mind, it gives rise to the illusory notion, "Whatever is inside my skin is 'me,' and whatever is outside is 'others.'"

This false notion results in emotions like anger, fear, hatred, depression, resentment, and frustration that are rampant in the challenging environment of Earth-life.

When we entertain such negative emotions in ignorance of our true nature, we resist the flow of life. Negative, hurtful memories, fixations about people, bitterness, and blame, choke the free flow of life within us. Eventually, this affects our physical, mental, and social wellbeing.

Whenever we entertain negative feelings about something or someone, whether we have felt hurt by others or caused others to feel hurt, a karmic scar gets etched on the whiteboard of pure consciousness. Consciousness gets stained by these impressions. We get bound by these scars.

Since most people are unaware this is happening, they keep accumulating many such scars of bondage. As a result, the universal consciousness that permeates the world becomes polluted. As this happens in the invisible realm, people find it difficult to believe. When we resist the free flow of life, we experience testing situations, limitations, and sorrow. This is the manifest form of karmic bondage.

We will understand how exactly karmic bondage gets formed and how it affects our lives in more detail in the next chapter.

4

Understanding Karmic Bondage

We all seek to experience lasting love, joy, peace, and completeness. We spend our lives pursuing them, and many of us leave the world never having found them. Indeed, it is a paradox that these experiences we pursue during our Earth-life are inherent qualities of our true nature, the Self. Then, why do we keep seeking something that we already essentially are?!

Most people would answer in the negative if they are asked whether they are satisfied with the state of their life – be it physical, mental, social, financial, or spiritual. They struggle to keep good health, harmonious relationships, financial stability, emotional wellbeing, and spiritual maturity. What holds them back from making progress?

Imagine some kids enjoying fireworks. One of them lights a firecracker rocket that propels towards the sky and bursts into many colors. When the rocket is lit, its natural tendency is to go skyward;

the laws of physics ensure that this happens. But what if the kid ties the rocket to a wooden stump on the ground with a strong chord and then lights it? Try as it may, the rocket will never be able to rise.

Apply this metaphor to our lives. Like the laws of physics, nature always ensures that everything contained within it constantly evolves toward a higher state of being. In this evolved state, we attain the perfect balance in all the five planes: physical, mental, social, financial, and spiritual.

Then, what holds us back? What is the wooden stump that is tethered to our being that withholds us? Karmic bondage!

Just like the rocket tethered to the ground, the unseen chords of our karmic bondages withhold us from unfolding our true potential. These bondages infest our thoughts and extend into our speech and actions. Such actions cause further bondage and distortion in our lives. We begin to fall out of tune with nature and lead an unconscious life. Had these chords of bondages been visible, it would have been easier to convince people of the importance of severing them.

What should we do to break out of this vicious cycle?

Firstly, we need to elevate our awareness and develop our understanding of how karmic bondages are formed and manifest in our lives. With an elevated awareness and the torch of understanding, we will refrain from creating further karmic bondages through our thoughts, feelings, speech, and actions.

Secondly, we need to break free of the past that weighs down on our present. We should cleanse our body-mind of the karmic scars that bind us to lowered awareness and ignorance. Just like an immaculate piece of sculpture that remains when everything else is chiseled away, we *are* the pure consciousness that remains when karmic scars are chiseled off. In the further chapters, we will discuss the tools that can be used to annihilate the karmic scars.

As we begin working on cutting off the bondages, we gradually emerge from the cycle of creating more bondages. We get attuned with nature and are intuitively guided with the exact thing to do every time.

The pillars of karmic bondage

A large part of solving any problem lies in understanding the problem itself. Once we understand the pillars on which a problem stands, it becomes easy for us to solve it. The same applies to karmic bondage too. Let's understand this with the help of an example.

Once, a villager had trouble falling asleep at night. A peculiar fear had gripped his mind. Whenever he lay on his bed for the night, he would feel that there was someone under his bed. He would often get up and peep under the bed to allay his fears. But again, when he would return to bed, he would find it difficult to fall asleep. He tried to change beds, but the problem remained. He visited doctors who suggested medications. He saw psychiatrists who tried to help him with his fears. In desperation, he even visited quacks and astrologers who claimed to have solved far more severe problems. But try as he may, he couldn't get any help with his predicament.

One day, fed up with his sleepless trepidation, he decided to get to the bottom of it by himself. He determinedly pondered his fear and concluded that his fear was mainly because of the space underneath his bed. If there hadn't been any space, there would be no fear! Then, as if the solution had struck him like lightning, he dashed out of his house, returned with a saw, and chopped off the four legs of the wooden bed. With the legs gone, there remained no space under the bed. After a long time, he slept like a baby!

A simple understanding cured the fear that not even doctors and psychiatrists could help with. He cut off the very pillars on which his fears stood. The same applies to karmic bondages. Once we understand the four pillars that prop our bondages, we can work on severing them.

We will discuss these four pillars in detail in the following chapters.

5

The Pillars of Karmic Bondage

We will now understand the four pillars that lead to karmic bondages. Let us denote these pillars by the fingers of our hand: the index finger, middle finger, ring finger, and the little finger.

The size of each finger also indicates the severity of their impact on our wellbeing. For example, the pillar indicated by the little finger has the least significant impact, while the pillar represented by the middle finger impacts our lives the most.

Let us begin with the most important pillar indicated by the middle finger.

The middle finger – Our karmic account

Our karmic account is a way of perceiving our bondage with everyone else. It is an invisible account that works like a bank account, except that it holds karmic impressions instead of money. The impressions formed by our thoughts, feelings, speech, and actions are stored in this account. Our goal is to reconcile and settle our karmic account.

A deposit is made into our karmic account whenever we think, feel, speak, or act negatively with anyone, intentionally or unintentionally. If we have caused people to feel hurt, insulted, angry, or pained, we have created a karmic scar, which gets deposited into our karmic account. Conversely, if anyone causes us to feel hurt, a karmic scar can be created unless we receive it gracefully and let it pass without reacting. Whenever we feel hurt by people or situations, we should remember that we are only receiving a payback from our own karmic account.

We often blame people or situations for hurting us without realizing that the hurtful scene has come only as an opportunity to release the scars from our own karmic account. People who seem to hurt us serve as a courier to deliver our karmic paybacks to us. Why should we blame the courier service? We should rather be grateful to them for delivering our paybacks, giving us the opportunity to settle our karmic account.

When we remain vigilant in hurtful situations and receive our karmic paybacks gracefully, we not only get rid of our past bondage but also avoid creating any new bondage for the future.

Let us understand how this works with an example.

Jay and Samir are neighbors. One day, Jay said something insulting to Samir about his old car. Now, Samir needs to understand that the insult that has come his way is arising from his own karmic account. He can respond to this situation in two ways. He may either accept the insult gracefully and choose not to retaliate, or he can retort to Jay in the same coin.

If he chooses to receive the insult gracefully, his karmic account gets reconciled to that measure. By not retaliating, he ensures that his karmic account is not renewed with fresh scars.

But if he retaliates, he makes a new deposit of insult into his karmic account. Instead of gracefully accepting something that nature sent him from his own account and settling it, his retaliation renews the account, and the bondage continues.

This is like saying, "See you again!" to the situation because the insult will return to him later, not necessarily through Jay, but perhaps through some other close acquaintance. When the same scene recurs, Samir will again have the choice of settling the account or renewing it.

From this example, we learn that we set the stage for future repetition of the same scene when we do not receive our karmic payback gracefully. This shows that we are not learning our lessons. If a particular undesirable scene keeps repeating in our life, it could mean that we lack the awareness and understanding to receive our paybacks gracefully and achieve closure.

The other point is that karmic bondage is never created one-to-one between two specific people or groups. So, if Samir received the payback of insult through his neighbor Jay this time, it could be through his boss the next time. Thus, nature finds the easiest possible route to deliver paybacks to us. And hence, most of the paybacks we receive are invariably through our near and dear ones. So, we may frequently feel hurt in our interactions with friends and family. Now, does that ring a bell?

The above example was just about a particular karmic scar in Samir's account that got triggered when it matured and presented itself. All these bondages, although unseen, weigh heavily on our life, keeping us from attaining peace, assurance, confidence, and fortitude.

Imagine the countless scars we may be creating every day by how we think or feel about people around us. To understand the subtlety of this topic, consider yourself stuck in a bad traffic jam. You're already late to reach your workplace, and the traffic is causing further delay. You feel a surge of stress and frustration within. Just then, someone tries to cut into the lane you're driving on or rushes past you, driving very close to your car or bike, just missing by inches, or scratching your vehicle, making you jump.

What do you do? If you instinctively curse the person as he passes by, you create a karmic scar. Even though you don't know him, and he also doesn't know that you just cursed him, karmic bondage is created, nonetheless.

The sudden unsettling fear you felt when the other traveler cut into your lane came from your karmic account. Nature delivered your payback through his medium to settle your account. When you face the situation with this understanding, receive it gracefully, and respond with discernment, you avoid renewing the karmic account with a negative reaction.

Nature constantly helps us by steering us towards clearing our karmic account. It keeps sending paybacks, hoping we would understand and clear them by gracefully receiving them. Indeed, life on Earth is a marvelous system that helps us heal ourselves and make progress.

This facet of scars that we have deposited in our karmic account and the paybacks we receive from our karmic account constitute the first pillar of karmic bondage. Since it is denoted by the middle finger, which is the longest finger, it accounts for most of our karmic bondage.

The ring finger – Present-day karmic scars

We create present-day karmic scars with people we meet on an ongoing basis. This may involve our immediate relatives, colleagues, friends, neighbors, etc. While interacting with them, we often think, feel, say, or do negative things that affect them and us.

We can consider these scars as karmic fingerprints we leave in their lives, just like the fingerprints an offender leaves at the crime site. After committing a crime, he escapes to a far-off city before the site of crime is investigated. But he feels anxious and terrified all the time because of his fingerprints.

Similarly our karmic fingerprints do not allow us to rest peacefully. Something always keeps tugging at us. We feel restless and dissatisfied for no apparent reason. This could probably be the play of the present-day karmic scars we keep etching habitually due to our tendencies.

The little finger – Ancestral karma

Our ancestors and their karma affect our lives to some extent. The overall impact of ancestral karma on our life is lesser than the other pillars. Hence, this pillar is denoted by the little finger.

It is generally accepted that, both genetically and karmically, the reach of ancestors extends for many generations. Theories have been postulated that each person inherits memories and tendencies from their ancestral lineage through their DNA. This could be the reason why some people instantly grasp and master skills at a very young age or recall knowledge of topics they have never formally learned.

The downside of the ancestral transfer of traits is the inheritance of negative impressions. Ancestral karmic scars have a harmful effect on our lives. They withhold us from realizing our full potential. We need to get rid of the karmic burdens caused by our ancestors that weigh down on our present.

For example, some people may feel inexplicable fears caused by emotional or physical trauma experienced by an ancestor. Some people may have an unexplained fear about not having enough to eat or a tendency to overindulge in food. Their ancestors might have been obsessed with hoarding and binging on food.

Some people may fear a shortage of money and a feeling that there is never enough to take care of their children. This could be because their ancestors grew up in financially challenging conditions. They would have had to work hard even for a meager amount of money and suffered from a constant feeling of scarcity.

If our ancestors have knowingly or unknowingly hurt others, they have incurred karmic bondages. The resentful feelings of the victims can deepen those karmic scars and have a telling effect on our lives too.

Thus, whatever negative impressions have been passed from our ancestors to us can cause difficulties for us in the present and keep us from living our life to the fullest.

We have discussed three pillars of karmic bondage – the middle, ring, and little fingers. In the next chapter, we shall discuss the fourth pillar that causes karmic bondage.

6

Karmic Bondage Due to Injured Memories

We have discussed the three pillars of karmic bondage in the previous chapter. Let's now understand injured memories—the fourth pillar of karmic bondage, denoted by the index finger.

Everyone is a storehouse of pleasant, painful, or neutral memories. We will focus on painful or injured memories as their effect on us is far more critical and harmful.

The index finger – Injured memories

Imagine you have a wound somewhere on your body that causes constant pain or burning sensation. When you are busy, you forget about it, but as soon as you focus on it, you feel the pain again.

In the same way, injured memories are like unhealed wounds that, whenever recalled, make us feel disturbed and restless. They evoke emotions like anger, hatred, jealousy, sorrow, depression, guilt, remorse, and fear. We may also experience physical symptoms such as a constant feeling of heaviness in the chest, sweating, a feeling of heat in the face, or tightness in the limbs.

Our SOUL purpose is achieved only when we heal our injured memories. However, since not many people know about injured memories, they traverse through life without healing them.

There are mainly two kinds of injured memories. The first kind of memories comes from our experiences during this lifetime. For example, the trauma caused by an accident during childhood precipitates as an injured memory. The victim inflicted with the injured memory either avoids encountering it or reacts in ways that aggravate it.

The second kind of injured memories is subtler to grasp. Each of us is born with some injured memories planted within us.

To understand how and why these memories are planted within us, we need to understand who is really born and the truth about re-birth.

The missing link in understanding reincarnation

The concept of reincarnation considers that life follows a cyclical pattern, offering the opportunity for learning and growing over many lifetimes. Life is seen as an opportunity to make continuous progress towards fulfilling its highest purpose.

According to this concept, the individual soul carries forward the essence of experiences and lessons learned from each lifetime and moves on to new births. In this process, the soul grows from the collective experiences from several lifetimes.

Another rationale behind the concept of reincarnation is renewal. With the onset of physical age, the human body wears out and becomes incapable of taking up fresh challenges and learning new lessons. Re-birth offers the soul a new embodiment to continue its learning and growth.

However, re-birth makes sense only when viewed from the limited standpoint of a separate individual, without considering the bigger picture. Let us understand this with the help of an analogy.

Suppose you place your hand in a pot to feel what's inside. Each finger touches a different thing. One finger touches mud; another touches a flower petal. A needle pricks the third finger while the fourth finger feels the softness of cotton wool. Each finger gets a different experience.

But who is really deriving all these experiences? Do these experiences belong to the fingers? No. You have placed your hand in the pot to derive all these experiences. While being outside the pot, you receive all the experiences *through* your fingers.

The fingers in this analogy represent human bodies, the pot represents the world, and the hand outside the pot represents the Self. Man feels that he is experiencing the various colors of life. But the Self, present beyond the world, is experiencing everything. He is the wise father who has sent his children as human embodiments to gather a diverse range of experiences from Earth-life. The Self acts through all bodies, and also receives the fruit of all actions.

When we understand the standpoint of the Self, re-birth loses its meaning. The Self exists before the body's birth and even after its death. The physical body is like a house. Houses are built, inhabited, and demolished. If one looks at life from the perspective of the house (body), there is construction (birth) and demolition (death). But there is no birth or death for the Self who builds, uses, and destroys the house. So, it's a matter of perspective.

Returning to the analogy, the experiences gathered through the fingers are stored in a memory pool. Suppose one of the fingers perishes. Consider that the hand grows another finger inside the pot. The one outside the pot re-uses the experiences of the perished finger from the memory pool and plants it in the new finger.

In other words, experiences gathered by the Self through all human bodies are available as a pool of memories. The Self re-uses certain memories gathered from one human lifetime by planting them in further bodies.

When these memories play out in the new body, the individual (the finger) cannot relate to them and hence considers them as his personal past-life memories. The truth is that all births are of the Self alone, just as all fingers belong to the hand outside the pot.

Healing of injured memories and progressive evolution

Why does the Self gather experiences and re-use them in new bodies? It is for healing them and bringing about progressive evolution. Every new generation is more advanced than the previous generation because of the re-use of memories by the Self.

There are child prodigies who demonstrate wondrous skills early in their childhood. We see instances of three-year-olds playing the piano skillfully, and kindergarten children easily solving complex mathematical problems. Scientists are baffled as they cannot explain this rationally.

Someone who is unaware of this game of the Self will assume himself as the re-birth of a previous human body.

The memory pool also contains injured memories of pain and trauma, fear and suffering endured through the multitudes of bodies. The Self plants such injured memories in new bodies for healing.

Consider a special type of refrigerator that not only preserves the food stored in it but also freshens it. If we place stale food in this refrigerator tonight, it will be fresh and healthy tomorrow morning.

Whether such refrigerators are available in the market is immaterial, but the human body can be considered as such a refrigerator. The Self has placed injured or traumatic memories in our bodies to heal and bring completion.

These injured memories get triggered and surface in response to certain situations. However, when we assume that we are separate individuals (fingers of the hand in the analogy), we are troubled by the pricking experiences that come our way. We take these memories personally without realizing that the Self has planted them only for healing and release.

Man keeps grumbling that his life is full of suffering. He keeps complaining: "Why me! Why am I going through such bitter experiences? I have helped my people, but no one helps me."

He should be asked, "Who are you?" The separate individual is a false notion. All the experiences are of the Self alone. If he helps his neighbor, it is like one finger helping its neighboring finger. When this topic becomes clear, one realizes that the hand is helping itself through the interplay of all its fingers. All help is Self-help!

When we are denied help, it is an opportunity to learn, mature, and evolve to a state where we realize ourselves as the source of love and compassion.

It can be truly liberating, when one contemplates this paradigm shift and builds conviction on it. All the suffering and grudges that we hold can vanish if this truth is understood.

7

The Memories-to-Lessons Connection

In the previous chapter, we have seen that the purpose of re-using memories is to heal them. Now, we will understand the most effective means of healing injured memories.

Memories achieve healing when we learn the lessons associated with them. A lesson could be about experiencing and expressing positive qualities like love, peace, happiness, courage, faith, trust, patience, forgiveness, kindness, creativity, empathy, etc., in contrasting or unfavorable circumstances. In this book, we will refer to them as SOUL lessons, because they help us achieve our SOUL purpose.

The experience of Earth-life is a contrast between ups and downs, pleasure and pain, joy-sorrow, good-bad, love-hate, anger-peace, faith-distrust. The range of experiences this contrast offers is rich and vast. We learn most when pushed into challenging situations.

Co-creation in Earth-life

Suppose a child wants to play cricket but has no one to play with. He insists his father should play with him. Although, his father is not interested, he agrees, because he loves his child and doesn't want to dishearten him.

The child likes to bat and wants to improve his game to get selected for his school team. What will the father do? Of course, he'll bowl so his darling child can practice batting! Not that he likes to bowl, but he will still do so out of love for his child.

The father wants him to improve his game and get selected for higher league matches. Hence, he bowls bouncers and googlies at his child. The child feels let down when he cannot face his father's bowling effectively and protests that his father is being unfair. He even complains that his father doesn't love him, making batting difficult for him.

The father then lovingly explains that he is raising the game's difficulty level so that his son can become an expert at batting. He can then hit the ball out of the ground with confidence without being flustered by the bouncers or googlies. He teaches his son to read the bowling carefully so that he can hit the ball for fours and sixes.

When the child learns the art of getting on top of the bowling and batting with confidence, he feels grateful for his father's contribution to his success.

In the game of cricket, you need someone to bowl so that you can bat. Without bowlers, you can never get to bat, and you won't be able to mature into an ace batsman.

This metaphorical game of cricket between father and son resembles the game of Earth-life. The father represents our relationships—our family, friends, neighbors, colleagues, managers, subordinates, our local civic services, and even the government! All these people, who play a variety of roles in our daily life, offer us the opportunity to mature and develop vital qualities like patience, uncompromising love, playfulness, persistence, resilience, creativity, and steadfastness, to name a few. Only when we develop these higher qualities, do we truly grow and mature and bring about a transformation within and around us.

When someone helps us in obvious ways, we feel they wish us well. However, when someone puts us down, constrains our progress, or poses hurdles in our life, we feel they are being unfair by bowling "real-life" bouncers and googlies at us.

We should consider people around us as partners, contributors, and co-creators in our life journey. Those who arouse contempt within us deserve our compassion. They play negative roles in our life only because they are co-creators.

When people push us to the edge, hurt or intimidate us, we should remember that in this Earth school, they are serving their worst only to bring out our best. They are co-creating our higher nature. We should recognize the negativity that others provoke within us as opportunities to introspect and invoke higher qualities.

Challenges in life are a doorway to growth. Every setback, frustration, obstacle, or struggle is a powerful teacher and an elevating springboard. This understanding helps us entertain only positive and happy thoughts even amidst struggles.

When we find that we are constantly locking horns with someone, it only means that they have some lesson for us that we are refusing to learn. We deny ourselves the opportunity to learn by either escaping or confronting them. With this understanding, we can stop denying and be open to receive our SOUL lessons. Life teaches through experiences that are co-created with those around us.

Understanding our SOUL lessons

Each of us is born with a certain set of SOUL lessons designed for us. Every person's syllabus is unique. Your lessons may not be meant for your spouse, siblings, or friends. You may find that they may be good at what you lack, and you may have perfected what they lack.

If a specific SOUL lesson is a part of your syllabus, it means that you are weak at it. You need to get better at it with constant practice. As we have discussed, nature helps us learn our SOUL lessons by surrounding us with people and situations that demand us to develop the quality that we are weak at. Let us understand this through some examples.

Consider a person whose SOUL lesson is Love. How would he behave? How would his life be? Since his lesson is love, he will be poor at it. He will find it difficult to express his love to the people around him. He may also feel less loved. He may firmly believe that he can experience love only when he receives it from others. Typically, he will be surrounded by people who exude hatred or contempt or cannot feel his love for them. They serve as co-creators for him to elevate the quality of selfless love and enable him to express love in a mature way.

Let us consider another example. Many people find it difficult to forgive others. Their SOUL lesson is Forgiveness. Nature helps them by surrounding them with people or situations that are unpardoning. They often land up in situations where they find it difficult to accept others. They get caught up in feelings of hatred, vengeance, or bitterness. Until they learn to forgive others and seek forgiveness themselves, such situations keep recurring in their lives.

Every problem or challenge is a blessing in disguise. Why? Because it invariably leads us to our SOUL lesson, which, when learned, gives us lasting peace and completeness. There are some methods that can be used to identify our SOUL lessons. In this book, we will call them as lenses. We will discuss these lenses in further chapters.

Someone whose SOUL lesson is Acceptance will find that she constantly resists life. She finds it difficult to accept things as they are. She may keep questioning, "Why me?", "Why this?", "What have I done to deserve this?" On introspection, she will find that she is rarely able to accept people or circumstances. She constantly encounters situations where her lack of acceptance causes her great sorrow and distress. Now, she can choose whether to take this hint and work upon herself or continue leading a life of struggle.

Faith is yet another SOUL lesson many of us are here to learn. Those who have Faith as their SOUL lesson find it difficult to trust others. They constantly doubt the intentions of those around them, even their immediate relatives. In contrast to them, we find some people who can innately trust people very easily. Naturally, faith is not their lesson. Their lesson could be discretion.

Patience is one of the most important lessons we are here to learn. Patience is a part of everyone's syllabus as it can be learned only during Earth-life. Lack of patience leads many people to commit blunders in their daily lives, leading to broken relationships, poor health, and complicated situations.

By identifying and learning our SOUL lessons, we can heal our injured memories because our injured memories are always connected to the lessons meant for us.

Let's explore the practical nuances of healing injured memories in the next part of the book.

PART 2

MANIFESTATION AND HEALING OF INJURED MEMORIES

8

The Self's Script for Healing and Growth

The divine and infinitely creative intelligence of the Self perpetually keeps scripting opportunities for healing, learning, and growth through the tapestry of human life. Let us understand this with the story of Dr. Amar.

Amar was a scientist involved in a research project on human DNA. Like many of those who achieve academic excellence, Amar had his share of flaws like a bloated ego, an air of self-righteousness, a tendency to compare and judge himself with others, and a habit of trumpeting his achievements.

During the advanced stages of the project, Amar began receiving threats from a rival group of scientists and industrialists who opposed his groundbreaking research. They started warning him of dire consequences and even threatened to kill him.

Amar was already under a lot of stress due to sleepless nights in his lab. Now he was finding it difficult to cope with the added stress of their threats and the fear of death looming over him. He felt paranoid that he could be killed at any time. To dodge his rivals, who were bent on destroying his research work, he decided to replicate his lab facilities at two other sites known only to him.

The rivals deployed a team of thugs, who set out to trace Amar's whereabouts. But Amar would stealthily move to his standby research labs just in the nick of time. In this way, though his attackers were hot on his heels, Amar managed to stay one step ahead and dodge them for several months. Every time he sensed being trailed, he kept escaping.

Imagine the feelings that Amar would be going through while working at his lab. The slightest sound of footsteps or a knock on the door would cause him to shudder. Imagine the stress and discomfort that was consuming him. On the one hand, he faced challenges with his research, leading to delays. On the other hand, death was looming over his head like the sword of Damocles.

Amar, a scientific thinker, was also assailed by many questions – "Why am I so scared of death? What is death? Is it the end? What lies beyond death? How can I overcome this fear? Have there been people who have successfully overcome their fear of death?"

Besides his research on human DNA, Amar began spending time seeking knowledge about death and the nature of emotions. All this was happening with a constant undertone of anxiety and fear. His research was hitting hurdles and results were not forthcoming. At the same time, his rivals were closing in on him.

Finally, on a rainy evening, Amar's assailants chased him as he was frantically escaping in his car. His car toppled from a bridge into the water below, and he was drowned to death.

***

Like Amar, we, too may feel overwhelmed by the challenges we face and the variety of emotions they trigger within us. But we need to remember that we are not experiencing anything new! The Universal Self has already experienced this entire range of emotions and vulnerabilities in the past through countless other bodies.

When we experience intense fear, we seek remedies. If we cringe and shrink in situations, we should contemplate, "Why am I withdrawing from the world? Why can't I live freely? I'm not the first to be fired from a job... I'm certainly not the first to find it hard to get the right match for marriage... Certainly, I'm not the only one to fail the exams... Countless people have failed job interviews but they have gone ahead and achieved extraordinary success... What's wrong with me?"

The grand plan of the Self is beyond the comprehension of the human intellect. The Self wants to explore something new through our body. It wants to overcome certain fears, conquer some weaknesses, and transcend some vulnerabilities that arise from memories.

We keep thinking, "This is my problem... My work is incomplete... My project is hitting roadblocks... Can my aspirations be fulfilled before I die? Will I ever be financially stable? When will I be able to travel around the world?" We hold so many worries and tensions. But when we look at life from the Self's perspective, all the stress of life's trials can dissolve. We can achieve lasting fulfillment if we understand our injured memories and start learning our SOUL lessons.

***

Amar's death is not the end of the story. The Self's divine plan is to heal the injured memories and incompleteness experienced *through* Amar's life by planting them in further bodies. This story will help us understand how Earth-life works for us. So, what happened next in the story after Amar's death?

His unresolved memories were planted in Akbar's body. Akbar grew up in an erudite and open-minded family that was conducive for him to develop an open mindset. He grew up to be a sensible and intelligent student of science.

When in school, Akbar was eager to learn swimming. But when his father took him to the local swimming pool to teach him, Akbar started cringing and withdrawing from the pool. Every time his father took him inside the pool, he was frightened to death. His father tried to convince him that he would be safe in waist-deep water, but to no avail.

After returning home from the pool, Akbar pondered why he could not overcome the fear of drowning in water. By now, you would have realized what was ailing him.

Many of our unexplained fears are the product of unresolved memories that are planted within us. If we feel a soul-wrenching fear on encountering certain situations, it is probably the old karmic scars of the past that get triggered within us.

When we lack this understanding, our default response is to avoid whatever triggers such fear or discomfort within us like Akbar did. We try to escape tormenting circumstances, not knowing that we are sidestepping the very lessons that we were meant to learn. We are avoiding the very wounds we were designed to heal.

Akbar completed his post-graduation and Ph.D. in his favorite subject, Epigenetics. He would intuitively strike insights and derive inferences on how the characteristics of the human genome can be enhanced by editing DNA sequences. Any guesses why he was so deeply attuned to this line of research?!

Amar's unfinished work is now being completed through Akbar. You would have seen such children who are well versed in music or complex mathematics from childhood. They intuitively connect with their favorite activity at a deeper level. It's all the play of memories! The Self wants to progress through these bodies, whether it is music, mathematics, or genetics. Hence, it re-uses what has already been learned by planting proficient memories in new bodies.

This also shows that memories are not necessarily negative. The Self also re-uses positive memories that contain knowledge or skills for the purpose of progressive evolution.

Amar belonged to a Hindu family, but his memories are re-used in Akbar, who is born in a family of Muslim faith. This depicts that religious faiths are man-made constructs; they don't matter to the Self. For the Self, all bodies are the expression of the same Oneness. The differences between religions and sects are an outcome of the limitations of human thinking. Amar's memories could have possibly been planted in Anthony, born to devout Catholic parents!

Since childhood, Akbar was tormented by the fear of untimely death. He would feel insecure and tensed while working alone in the lab on the university campus during late evenings. Often, he would put his work aside and rush home as some unknown fear would grip him for no obvious reason.

Being an introvert and deeply curious about the truth of life and death, Akbar was attracted to spiritual discourses. He was delighted to gain the higher perspective of life beyond the mundane knowledge of the world. He learned about the fallacy of death and the eternal nature of the Self beyond life and death of the human body.

For Akbar, understanding of the SOUL purpose of life was a fear-shattering experience. Although he would never get to know the specific stories of the memories he had inherited, he learned that they were meant to be overcome and healed.

With deep observation and introspection, Akbar could detach himself from the emotions that troubled him. He developed an attitude of playfulness in the same situations that tormented him.

With the spiritual insights he gained, Akbar developed a feeling of peaceful assurance, "Even if I do not complete my research, I need not worry because no work is personal. Everything is happening according to the divine plan. Even if I cannot conclude this research, nature will ensure its continuity and culmination in the future. This process has been going on since eternity, and human consciousness is bound to progress to its pinnacle."

The more Akbar broke the shackles of his injured memories, the more intuitive and productive he became. His research work, a continuation of the good work done by Amar, gained momentum, and he could achieve a breakthrough in his research during his early thirties.

In this way, this knowledge helped Akbar eliminate both – the burden of completing his research and the fear of death. He could heal a significant part of the wounds he had embodied at birth.

***

Think about it. Would Akbar have embarked on the journey of self-discovery if he had not been troubled by the burden of fear and anxiety? Develop the conviction that the burdens of life are not actually burdens but an invitation to self-discovery, the inner calling for healing, and an opportunity for growth.

From the story of Amar and Akbar, we would have gained an insight into how memories play out across human incarnations in the pursuit of healing. In the next chapter, we will understand how injured memories manifest and our responses either heal or worsen them.

9

The Play of Memories – 1

We have understood that the creases and stains accumulated on the universal consciousness through one human body are cleansed and ironed through bodies that come later. With the help of some more examples, let us understand how injured memories are passed from one body to another and how the Self achieves healing.

***

On learning that he had failed his exams in school, Neel returned home with a sad heart. But he was more frightened than sad. He feared breaking this news to his father but did not resort to lies. He truthfully approached his father and showed him his school progress report. His father was already distraught about a difficult situation at work. On hearing the news of Neel's failure, he got furious and started beating him. Neel tripped, and his head hit the sharp edge of the study table. He died before reaching the hospital.

What was the predominant thought in Neel's mind when he died? He would have regretted speaking the truth. For him, his uprightness led to his death. Now, the boy's memories are planted in a girl, Leena.

Ever since Leena started going to school, she had a tendency to lie to feel secure. She would feel restless when her parents and teachers demanded her to speak the truth. She didn't know why she felt nervous about revealing her mind. She remained secretive about her feelings and actions. She resorted to deceit to protect herself from the fear of divulging her inner truths, thereby creating complications in her life.

We can now understand that the Self has planted Neel's injured memory in Leena's body for healing. This also suggests that the Self does not go by gender while planting memories. Memories gathered from a man's body can be planted in a girl and vice versa. The gender of the human body is a façade that is immaterial to the purpose of healing. A man can embody feminine qualities, while a woman can embody and demonstrate masculine qualities. We need to rise above our fixations about gender differences.

Leena needs to muster the courage to overcome her unexplained fear of being forthright and truthful. Courage and honesty are her SOUL lessons. She may choose to avoid her fear by trying to justify why deceit is essential to survive in the world. Alternatively, she can decide to encounter her fears. Her fear begins to heal when she dares to be upright and sincere in communicating with people.

And what happened to Neel's father? He spent the rest of his life plagued by guilt for what happened to Neel. He kept blaming and punishing himself for the regretful episode. After his demise, whoever inherited his painful memory is prone to experience deep guilt from childhood. They will live life in fear of hurting others at the cost of hurting themselves. Another unfinished business of Neel's father was his lack of patience, which led to his reckless reaction towards Neel. The one who inherits his memory can be impulsive and prone to outbursts. Patience and Forgiveness are the SOUL lessons to be learned to heal his memories.

***

A soldier was on duty patrolling the border. After his scheduled sleep hours, he woke up at dawn and got out of his bunker to catch some fresh air. As he stretched his hands skyward and yawned, he did not realize that he was the target of a rifle trained at him from across the border. He was shot dead in an instant.

For the soldier, stretching out and opening himself to the surroundings had invited his death. How would the injured memory of this soldier play out in a new body? The body that inherits this memory would always shrink and withdraw. He will feel uncomfortable opening up and expressing himself. This memory will manifest as stage fear, fear of expressing oneself in a crowd, and constricted body movements.

***

David had just landed a job in an engineering company that manufactured machine tools. As he was determined to prove himself at his new job, he started working long and late hours. His mother was in the advanced stage of a disease and used to complain about severe pain. She begged David to take her to a good doctor.

David ignored her frequent pleas as he spent most of his time in his office, even on weekends. His mother's condition deteriorated over the next six months, and she eventually died. David couldn't pardon himself when the doctor explained how her illness had turned fatal. He lived with the guilt of not having balanced his time between work and home to care for his mother.

He remained a bachelor for the rest of his life and died in a road accident when he was forty years old. His feeling of incompleteness at failing to care for his mother was an injured memory.

David's injured memory was inherited by Anita, who was born into an affluent family. She graduated in fine arts and married Rohan at the young age of twenty-one. After fifteen years of their marriage, Rohan suffered a severe stroke, leaving his left side paralyzed.

As Rohan was bed-ridden, Anita had no other option but to dedicate herself to caring for him. She took care of all his needs and fed and cleaned him. When she found time out of her daily chores, she would read books aloud to him. She would often wonder how fate had played with their lives. However, she never shied away from her caregiver role for Rohan. She loved him dearly and did everything possible to make his life comfortable.

We can see that David's unfulfilled memories could achieve fulfillment through Anita's life as a caregiver. What David didn't do for his mother, Anita did for her husband, healing the injured memories.

Instead of accepting her situation gracefully and serving Rohan happilly, what if Anita had fretted and complained about her situation and found ways to avoid her role as a caregiver? She would have aggravated the karmic bondage and left the memory unhealed.

***

Many people feel restless and claustrophobic upon on entering a lift or a closed cabin. For unexplainable reasons, they feel they will not survive. This could be due to the memory of a prior death in a constrained environment, like being trapped under debris of a collapsed building or being burried alive.

Many of us also have fear of heights. We tremble even considering standing on the terrace of a high-rise building. This could also be due to a painful memory of a fall from a high altitude.

Some people feel terrified when they have a minor illness or if they have to be admitted in a hospital. The fear of death hovers on their mind. Even if the illness can be easily cured, the person remains jittery and anxious through the illness. The possible reason could be the painful memories of someone battling a terminal illness in a hospital, feeling the onset of death every moment while being bed-ridden.

Betrayal is yet another trauma that causes intensely painful memories. A man wins over someone's love and trust and then betrays them. Someone usurps a sibling's wealth or becomes an infidel, a serpent posing as a benefactor. The jolt of betrayal causes a painful memory. If the Self re-uses such a memory in a new embodiment, the receiver of this memory will find it extremely difficult to trust people. They may even find it difficult to warm themselves to people who love them. Love and Faith are their important SOUL lessons.

***

With the help of the above examples, we can introspect our life and get a vague idea of the kind of memories that are waiting to be healed through us.

We have discussed various scenarios where nature heals injured memories by re-using them. But nature's ways are not directly perceptible to human understanding. In the next chapter, we will look at how the intricate work of healing happens, unknown to us, with the story of a truck driver.

10

The Play of Memories – 2

Madan was a middle-aged man who used to earn a living by driving a truck for a goods transport company. He had a habit of drunk driving. Being an alcoholic and a driver is a deadly combination. All his friends warned him against his addiction. They told him how dangerous his habit was, not only for himself but also for others on the road. But he paid no heed to his friends. He felt that he could drive confidently and safely even after consuming alcohol.

One evening, while driving drunk on his usual route, Madan lost control of his truck and ran over a farmer walking by the roadside. The poor farmer was killed in the accident, and Madan was arrested. During the investigation, the police officials found that he was drunk and concluded that the accident was entirely his fault. A criminal case ensued. The presiding judge was a person with a spiritual bent of mind. After hearing the pleas and witnesses, he passed a surprising and unusual sentence.

The farmer was survived by his parents, wife, and two children in a little village. The farmer had some enemies who were trying to snatch his farmland. The justice by the judge was that Madan should live with the farmer's family for ten years. He should work and earn for them, feed and protect them, given that their sole bread earner and protector was dead. The judge warned Madan that if he tried to escape, every such attempt would double the term of his sentence. Madan was disappointed at the loss of his freedom but was relieved as his life was spared.

As the root cause of the accident was Madan's alcoholism, the judge ordered him to join a rehabilitation center and get rid of his addiction, after which he was deputed to the farmer's village.

As sentenced by the judge, Madan moved to the farmer's village and started living with the farmer's family. The family hated the very sight of Madan. They could not bear that the very culprit responsible for the farmer's death was now living with them under the same roof. At lunch and dinner, they would throw his bread at him. They would abuse him whenever they encountered him in the house or on the street. The farmer's wife would not even look at him.

Madan felt sad and angry with their behavior. He was growing tired of their hatred and started abusing them in return. When they would throw the bread on his plate, he would push the plate away and refuse to eat. He would sulk for hours and deliberately not help with anything at home or in the farm. Even if someone needed help, he would ignore it. Such behavior made it even more difficult for him to gain their approval.

But how long could he starve? Eventually, hunger trumped anger, and he mellowed down. He tried to escape once but was caught and brought back, and his sentence doubled to twenty years. He felt utterly trapped, helpless, and desperate. He could neither escape nor could he bear to stay. Once caught, even the thought of escape frightened him as it would amount to doubling his already lengthy sentence.

Many people find themselves in such helpless situations where they can neither escape nor bear to stay. If they gracefully accept what is served on their plate and have faith in nature's way, they will soon see that whatever they were forced to go through was for their own greatest good.

Being bored of just sitting idle, Madan started doing small household chores as the days passed. He also began visiting the farm and learned farming. Gradually his efforts bore fruit. Inspired by the results, he was motivated to work harder, and soon the farm had a healthy crop. He learned to protect his farm from heavy rains and severe droughts. He also fought robbers who tried to steal his crop. His farming activities began to bring a steady income to the farmer's family.

After nearly five years of hating him for killing their son, the farmer's parents developed some sympathy and liking for him. He even began helping the farmer's school-going son with his studies. Gradually the children also started liking him. Soon, everyone in the house began liking him except the farmer's wife.

One day, when the farmer's enemies attacked the family in the dead of night, Madan came to their rescue and saved the family. He fought the enemies and got them arrested, thus putting the family out of danger. After being saved by Madan from what was certain death, the farmer's wife also felt grateful to him, and she finally accepted him as her brother. The woman who had not spoken to him for all these years not only accepted him as her brother but even felt happy in his company.

This gave Madan a great sense of satisfaction and completeness. From that day, though he stayed at the farmer's house, it never felt like a punishment anymore.

***

Madan's recklessness, abusive nature, and guilt of killing the farmer were manifestations of the injured memories planted in him. These memories needed healing and completion. Every incident he faced, including the accident with the farmer, was nature's arrangement to help him heal all the incompleteness within him.

Being spiritually oriented, the judge knew that Madan needed to heal his incompleteness, and the perfect way to achieve it was for him to stay with the farmer's family. The bereaved family would be an ideal setting for him to get rid of his impurities and heal himself. In hindsight, we can see that the judge's decision was perfect.

Feeling helpless and desperate, Madan accepted his situation and came to terms with what he should have done in the first place – working and caring for the farmer's family. With this, he began finding solutions to his problems, and he felt more and more satisfied. This continued to a point where he attained purity and completeness. The sentence, which was supposed to be a punishment, didn't now matter to him!

In the next chapter, we will look at another version of this story with an alternate course of events.

11

The Play of Memories – 3

Let us now consider an alternate course of events to Madan's story. The same accident happened. However, this time, both Madan and the farmer died. As it happened, the farmer's wife, who was pregnant, gave birth to a baby boy shortly after his death.

Here, the situation passed out of the hands of the judge into the hands of nature! In the earlier version of the story, the judge meted out justice to Madan, who committed the crime. So, the justice was person-oriented. However, the justice of nature is based on memories. Every injured memory must be healed. It is not important who inherits the memory but that it should be healed.

Madan's injured memories could have been healed by staying with the farmer's family, but they remained unhealed because of his death. So, nature found the next best way to heal these memories by placing them in Aakash, the dead farmer's newborn boy! The purpose was to plant them in the person staying with the family – and who better than Aakash was worthy of healing them.

So, Aakash was born with Madan's injured memories. The farmer's wife hated and cursed Aakash, considering him an inauspicious omen for their family. "His father had to die for him to be born," alleged his mother. Everyone else in the family, his siblings, and grandparents, had a similar perspective about him. They all hated him.

As Aakash grew older, he began to question, "Why does everyone hate me? Why does my mother curse me? Why doesn't anyone care for me and understand my feelings?" He did not understand why he was being ill-treated. He hadn't done anything wrong to deserve this.

Many of us often do not understand why certain events happen to us. We are thrust into a testing situation that we find unbearable for no logical reason. We find no explanation for the discomfort or insecurity we feel in certain circumstances. Very often, we may also feel that we don't deserve the pain that we have to bear. These could be manifestations of the injured memories placed within us.

Coming back to Aakash's story, as he grew up, he became unhappy with the treatment he received and started abusing everyone. At the age of eighteen, he tried to escape twice but was traced and brought back.

Note that whether it is the justice done by the judge or nature, the same events were happening in the alternate version of the story. But here, Aakash was unaware of why everyone hated him.

He prayed for help and freedom in his desperation. As an answer to his prayers, nature introduced him to a spiritual guru. Aakash asked the guru why he was being ill-treated and the possible solution to his problems.

The guru guided him to practice forgiveness. As a part of the practice, he had to forgive and seek forgiveness from others. Aakash was surprised at his advice. "Why? What have I done that I should seek forgiveness?" And it seemed logical too. If he hadn't done anything wrong, why should he seek forgiveness?

The guru revealed what no one else had told Aakash. He explained, "There is a lingering incompleteness within you that is seeking completion. Your body is like a house you have been given to live in. But before you can fully live in it, you must clean it. Resolving your incompleteness is like cleaning the house before living in it. If you continue to live in a dirty house, the experience of living in it will not be the best."

Aakash went through similar experiences as Madan did in the earlier version of the story. As he worked and cared for his family, the doors to completion were gradually thrown open for him. He was soon absolved of his sorrows and attained purity and completeness.

But for this to happen, Aakash had to gracefully accept the karmic paybacks of the injured memories and seek forgiveness even though he had no clue why all this was happening to him. Instead of resisting others, he had to forgive them for ill-treating him.

In the absence of the guru and his teachings, it was unlikely that Aakash would have done this. He would have continued to respond with a vengeance, repeat his mistakes and grow up with contempt for all his relatives. He would have regarded them as his enemies.

***

How do you win over an enemy? Not by killing them, but by befriending them! Anyone we see as an enemy is actually helping us attain purity and completion. They are part of nature's arrangement. Our negative response to that person can never lead us to completion.

For example, one who is trying to heal anger will be constantly exposed to people who make him angry. He will regard such people with contempt and hate them. Instead, he should thank them in his mind, if not in person. They are helping him attain purity and completion by getting rid of his anger.

The notion that others are not enemies, but friends go a long way to help us respond to them in the right way. Whether we know what our lessons are or not, considering someone an enemy and responding negatively does not help. Understanding this is a great step towards our ultimate goal.

"Howsoever others behave, I always choose a happy response. Happiness is not the effect of my response but the cause of it. I will respond not because I seek happiness but because I *am* happiness!" This attitude can go a long way in achieving healing and completion.

Often, we find it difficult to accept the pain and burden of life. We may feel frustrated about why we have to put up with all the baggage of injured memories. The next chapter discusses this predicament and offers insights to pacify our apprehensions.

12

We All Have Been Chosen

Born without hands and legs, Nick Vujicic knew from childhood that he was different. Having experienced bullying as a child, he fell into depression and even tried to drown himself at the age of ten.

In a complete turnaround of outlook towards life, Nick discovered that he was his biggest discourager. He stopped his self-sabotage and searched for a meaning to his life. He started using his disability as a springboard to motivate people.

Today, he is well known worldwide. He has delivered motivational speeches in more than fifty countries on inspiring self-transformation. In his words, "I am grateful for what I have rather than being angry for what I don't. God has given me grace, strength, and comfort through my disability. You can have victory, peace, and joy through your circumstances."

Think about it. Someone, who is born without limbs, could be easily weighed down by their physical challenges. But trailblazers like Nick show us how any challenge, no matter how grave, can be overcome to achieve peace, success, and fulfillment.

There are many such motivating life stories, like that of Helen Keller or Abraham Lincoln. They thrived despite all adversities, challenged the limitations they were born with and discovered great meaning in their lives. They left behind a legacy that continues to inspire people.

You would have heard people complaining, "God has wronged me. Why do I always get a raw deal? I have to put up with so much more suffering than others. Everyone else is enjoying their life."

The lives of people like Nick or Helen Keller are reassurance for those who feel this way. Life has never been unfair to us. We have never been at the receiving end of inequality or injustice. The truth is that the Self - the divine chooser - has rightly chosen us because He believes in us!

If you are suffering from a particular disease, you choose to go to a specialist doctor for treatment. You choose a computer expert to fix a problem with your computer. If you want to grow a home garden, you choose a horticulture specialist. You choose these people because you are confident of their expertise to complete the job perfectly.

Similarly, the divine chooser seeks to heal all kinds of injured memories. This work has constantly been going on since time immemorial. By divine inspiration, the chooser chooses the right body-mind that can be entrusted with a particular injured memory. He has full faith that such a body-mind can heal these injured memories. The body-mind is bestowed with healing power far greater than the severity of the injured memories planted in it. Let us understand this with an example.

A boy, who wants to visit a carnival, asks his father for some pocket money for his expenses. The father ponders, "How much will he need for the expenses? At the most, two hundred rupees. I'll give him three hundred. Let him keep an extra hundred rupees for any unforeseen need."

Similarly, Mother Nature has instilled surplus power in us to cope with our challenges and heal our memories. But when we forget that we are here to enjoy the Earth-carnival, even this surplus power may fall short. When people face numerous challenges, out of ignorance, they may aggravate their problems by drowning themselves in addictions like alcohol or indulging in self-sabotage.

If we remember the purpose of Earth-life, we can overcome life's challenges with the surplus power. This surplus power is redeemed by:

- Realizing who-we-truly-are beyond the body and mind.
- Understanding the purpose of Earth-life beyond the mundane goals of worldly life.
- Developing conviction that injured memories are not our personal memories. Our body-mind is only the means for healing them.

There is no reason to believe that something unfair is being done by instilling injured memories. Be assured that these memories that emerge within you have been consciously chosen by the Self.

Every material has a different melting point. We cannot expect iron to melt at room temperature. It must be heated to about 1500 degrees before it starts melting. Hence, iron is placed in a crucible made of a material, like ceramic, that can withstand temperatures higher than its melting point. If we want to melt lead, we only need to heat it to about 300 degrees, for which an iron crucible will do.

Similarly, to heal an injured memory of a particular kind and severity, it needs to be subjected to conditions that trigger it and bring it into our awareness. For this, the memory must be placed in the right container – the right body-mind that can withstand its melting point.

For example, to heal a particular traumatic memory, a disabled body is needed. No other body can heal this memory. A different kind of memory of hurtful arrogance can be healed only through a body born in a financially challenged family, where it must toil hard to earn bread. To heal another injured memory of reckless stupidity, a frail body prone to sickness can become essential.

So, the Self creates such bodies and plants those specific memories in them. What does one think when he is unable to accept his body-mind and circumstances? "Why was I born in such a poor family? Why did I have such miserly parents? Why have I got a body with such a complexion?" He is unaware of the perfect and elaborate arrangements that nature has made for his growth. He cannot imagine the bliss and contentment he can experience if he uses these arrangements appropriately.

If a student training in martial arts is told by his master to tie his right hand and practice only with his left hand, he may find it difficult and unreasonable. But the master has arranged suitable exercises for him to strengthen his weak and inflexible left hand.

In the same way, the arrangement of people and situations made for you is a cause for celebration! You have obtained your body exactly as the Self intends. Nothing is lacking in the body-mind for fulfilling its divine plan. Hence, when you accept the memories instilled within you with the attitude, "Thy wish is my will. Let Thy will be done," such devotion helps in healing.

There are such extraordinary souls who made higher choices despite all adversities. They made tough choices even though their emotions overwhelmed them. But without this knowledge, people prefer to stay in their comfort zone and earn sympathy by telling others about how they are suffering. They keep justifying their escapist behavior.

Hence, their injured memories do not heal. They may attain success in their careers and enjoy all the comforts. But if they do not work on their injured memories and learn their SOUL lessons, their life remains unfulfilled. They continue to feel incomplete within.

The discomfort you experience when these memories get triggered should not be taken as a burden but rather an opportunity. There is no need to stress yourself over the need to heal your injured memories. If it remains incomplete, the Self continues this process perpetually through new embodiments until it achieves complete healing. But efforts must be made from a relaxed state of mind to achieve healing to the extent possible during this Earth-life.

13

Confronting Karmic Scars

Computer programs are inactive when stored on disks. But when the computer is turned on and these programs are invoked, they come alive on the computer screen or in the background.

In many ways, the human mechanism is also like a set of memory programs brought to life in the presence of the Self. Memory programs get triggered in response to external events. They run within our body and manifest on the screen of life, either visibly in the external world or silently within the mind.

When an injured memory is formed, it is associated with a negative emotion that causes the karmic scar. For example, we feel angry if someone abuses us in a crowd. This causes a karmic scar that is lodged in this injured memory associated with anger.

Whenever this memory is recalled, the associated emotion also gets triggered. In the above example, if we happen to be in a crowd and someone starts scolding us, the earlier memory is recalled, and the associated emotion of anger is triggered. We all have karmic scars lodged within injured memories. They are like wounds inside our body-mind.

According to nature's arrangement, the people around us often provoke our wounds. Karmic scars that we have hidden away from the world are touched and reopened by our close ones like friends, relatives, and acquaintances.

The reopening of karmic wounds

We all have been in a situation where we have a painful wound on our body, say the fingers, the arm, or the feet. When someone bumps into us exactly on that painful spot, the wound reopens, sending spirals of intense pain through our body. Even though they may have done it unintentionally, we get upset with them. We even accuse them of purposely hurting us on the spot where we were already injured. This is also known as touching a raw nerve. The nerve is already painful, and someone presses it exactly at the point of pain, causing us to scream.

Suppose you have a fresh wound on your right-hand thumb, and your friend comes and shakes hands with you. It is a warm handshake for him, but it turns out to be a painful grip for you that makes you recoil. Your friend is unaware of the wound on your thumb that he has just aggravated.

Why do we get into situations where our karmic scars, both old and new, get bruised, more so by those close to us, whom we love and care?

As we are unaware that it is their divine role to do so, we curse, scold, and accuse them instead of thanking them.

Let us understand this with the help of an example:

Let's say we live in a house with many cracks in the wall of the drawing-room. We obviously do not want visitors to see these cracks. We feel ashamed to reveal the plight of the house to others. So, we seal the cracks with plaster.

One day, a guest bangs against the wall by accident, chipping away the plaster in some of the cracks. We feel embarrassed, fearing that the guest might notice the cracks. We become anxious that the cracks we worked so hard to hide from the world are now exposed.

Revealing the cracks isn't a big deal, but we take it to heart and feel pained. There is no reason for us to feel embarrassed about it. In fact, we can point out the cracks to the guests ourselves, "Look, there are cracks on the wall here. Please pray that we get a nice and beautiful home!"

This example shows that the pain, shame, or embarrassment we feel in this context is unnecessary. There are certain situations where it is justified to be embarrassed, and in others it is not. We should be able to differentiate between the two.

The home in the above example refers to our body-mind. The cracks in the walls refer to the karmic wounds we have concealed from the world. They are the karmic scars attributed to injured memories. The guest refers to the people around us or any situation in our life that inadvertently bruises these karmic wounds, causing us pain and shame.

The diamond hidden in every crack

If we knew what these cracks contain, we wouldn't react negatively to their opening. The truth is that every crack hides a diamond. Every time a crack opens, it is an opportunity for us to acquire that diamond! But we never give the diamond a chance to emerge from the crack.

The diamond is a SOUL lesson hidden in every karmic wound. Every karmic scar, every injured memory, holds within it a SOUL lesson to be unraveled. We should perceive every painful emotion, no matter how severe, as an opportunity to learn a lesson and grow. Whenever a person or a situation causes pain or sorrow, we must recognize that some karmic scar we suppressed and avoided, perhaps many years ago, has reopened.

Even as a child, we could have committed acts that we could not share with anyone. Later, we feel ashamed and try to cover up the wound to hide it from the world. In other words, the incident precipitates as an injured memory that leaves a karmic scar. **But we try to suppress the wound to escape the related memory, unwilling to face it.** Later in life, we encounter some person or situation that causes these old wounds to open. We feel hurt and embarrassed and try to suppress or escape them again.

If it is wrong to seal the crack by suppressing or escaping the injured memory, what is the right response? What should we ideally do when our karmic scars get triggered?

Nature has carefully placed diamonds in our home (our body-mind) while designing it. The opening of every crack takes us closer to these diamonds. It is as if every diamond contained in the cracks is eagerly waiting for us to find and retrieve it. And every diamond that we find and acquire adds to our spiritual affluence. We are all diamond collectors! It is in this pursuit we have descended on Earth. This is our Mission Earth! The success of our mission depends on the diamonds we collect while we are here.

Once we are firmly convinced that every injured memory holds a precious lesson, and every lesson that we embrace adds to the success of our Mission Earth, we will not shy away from confronting our painful memories.

How to respond when karmic scars are revived

When a new karmic scar is created, or an old scar is opened, we must tell ourselves that we don't need to conceal, escape, or suppress it. When our karmic scars get bruised by people or incidents, most of us either suppress the emotions or hurl them at others. Both kinds of reactions are harmful to us.

If we vent our anger, frustration, or resentment on others by scolding, abusing, or hurting them, people start disliking us, and our relationships lack harmony. No one wants to be with us if we keep hurting them for the issues we cannot handle ourselves.

On the other hand, if we suppress our emotions and put up a "good-looking" mask, people may probably like us because we appear peaceful to them and never let them know how we really feel. But the harmful effects of suppressing emotions would appear in the form of chronic diseases within us.

When we don't understand the right way to deal with our karmic scars, we respond to people and incidents in the same old ways, making matters worse for us and others. One scar can lead to many more scars, broken relationships, and karmic bondages. It becomes a spiral descent into a sorrowful life.

Every time an injured memory surfaces, we must feel it fully instead of trying to suppress or escape it. Of course, this may seem far more difficult than the other two alternatives until we practice and become proficient at it. When we stay put with an emotion and feel it completely without escaping, the SOUL lesson it holds gets revealed to us.

Once the diamond is acquired, the crack disappears. Learning the lesson heals the injured memory, and it no longer affects us. We will discuss this technique in the next chapter.

14

The Tools For Healing – 1

So far, we have discussed the SOUL purpose of life, the four kinds of karmic bondages, and the play of injured memories. We have also seen how injured memories hold the SOUL lessons we're meant to learn and how they are selectively planted in bodies best suited to heal them.

Let's now understand the tools for healing them. These tools are effective regardless of the kind of injured memories or emotions. The proof of the pudding lies in the doing! Hence, practicing them is more important than merely learning about them.

There are four powerful tools: the duster, the spectacles, the cutter, and the torch. Their vigorous and persistent practice can reveal wonders that will baffle the intellect! Let's now understand the duster and the spectacles.

The duster of forgiveness

People wonder why they feel drained of energy despite not doing much physical activity. They do not realize that being mean or merciless causes huge stress on them. It takes a lot of energy to exert anger or hatred towards those we believe have wronged us.

Blame or mercilessness can be directed either towards others or inward, taking the form of guilt. In either case, it creates karmic bondage. Since karmic bondage occurs at the mental level, karmic cleansing, too, needs to essentially happen at the mental level.

We can use the duster of forgiveness for this cleansing. True forgiveness involves releasing deeply held negative feelings. It empowers us to recognize the pain we suffered and enables us to heal and move on with our life without letting that pain define us.

Forgiveness is not just about seeking or accepting apologies. It has a deeper side to it. It involves love, compassion, sensitivity, and awareness. It wipes away the scars of hatred, resentment, and arrogance and purifies the mind. It brings us into alignment with God.

Wherever there is injury, there is hurt. Wherever there is hurt, there is the notion of a perpetrator – someone who has hurt us. However, the injured memories we have inherited from the universal memory are not our own experiences. In this case, the perpetrator is not known, but the associated emotions cause a burden on us. Forgiveness works wonders in healing these injured memories. It heals the wound and leads us to the SOUL lesson hidden in it.

The practice of forgiveness consists of three aspects:

- Seek forgiveness from all those who felt hurt.
- Forgive everyone who may have hurt us knowingly or unknowingly.

- Seek forgiveness from the Creator collectively for everyone, including us.

Forgiveness essentially works in the mental realm. Hence, we can sincerely seek forgiveness mentally within ourselves, with the people or situations related to our injured memories. We need not necessarily seek forgiveness by speaking to others in person, although we may do so if we feel comfortable.

It is not humanly possible to accurately identify the details of the injured memory and pinpoint the people who felt hurt or caused hurt. Hence, we can practice forgiveness with a heartfelt intent to principally address all those who may have been involved in forming the karmic scars. Our prayer for forgiveness touches and heals all the entities involved in the situation and the associated memories.

It is common for people to think, "Why should I seek forgiveness? How am I to be blamed for whatever has transpired before my birth? I have never hurt anyone. These memories are planted in me. If others were at fault, why should I own the responsibility?"

Seeking forgiveness does not mean we are being blamed for the karmic scars. It only means that we are a responsible presence willing to heal the negativity that plagues the collective psyche of humanity. We are gracefully taking responsibility to cleanse consciousness by erasing the karmic scars that appear in our awareness.

When we seek forgiveness, we are not judging others' actions. Instead, we are healing the situation and freeing ourselves from the karmic bondage that grips us. We seek forgiveness from the pure consciousness because it has been tainted. By practicing forgiveness for and on behalf of our ancestors, we can also wipe out our inherited karmic scars.

Use the duster of forgiveness to heal all karmic scars by offering the following prayer daily:

O God, please forgive me for all the karmic scars held within me.

Please forgive me for whatever contribution I have made to the problem through my feelings, thoughts, words, and actions.

Please forgive me for not recognizing your presence while harboring anger, resentment, hatred, and complaints.

Please forgive all of us who have contributed to this karmic bondage.

Thank you for freeing me and everyone else from bondage.

By consistently using the duster of forgiveness to wipe the karmic scars, we begin to feel unburdened and progress towards a state of purity and completeness.

The spectacles of detached witnessing

When people face uncomfortable emotions, they resort to the following two ways to get rid of them.

1. Expressing emotions on others

They spew their uncomfortable emotions on others by expressing their anger or resentment. With this, they may temporarily escape their discomfort and feel relieved, but it creates karmic scars. Hatred, envy, and anger ultimately burn them in the fire of regret. Anger may arise for any reason but always ends with regret and sorrow.

Further, those on whom they dump their negative emotions either distance them or look for opportunities to get even with them. Thus, they put the harmony in their relationships at stake.

2. Suppressing emotions

They suppress their emotions and may appear calm on the outside but simmer within. When they can no longer bear their suppressed feelings, they suddenly erupt like a volcano one day. The sustained suppression leads to diseases in the organs affected by those emotions.

We can see that both ways give only temporary relief. We must understand and practice the right way to achieve permanent freedom from karmic scars. Only then can we achieve healing and learn our SOUL lessons.

Witness emotions with detachment

The most effective way to be free from the grip of negative emotions is to observe them as a detached witness. Emotions are like storms raging in the ocean. They come and go. If you are alert and raise your awareness during the storm, you will learn the trick of detaching yourself from the emotions.

The trick is to neither express nor suppress but witness the emotions from a detached standpoint. Let us understand how such witnessing is possible.

When we observe our emotions, it may be difficult to detach from them initially, as we are habitually identified with them. A deep notion within us suggests that "All this is happening with me." Hence, emotions can overpower us.

However, the truth is that the emotions are not with us. They are with the body and mind. We are neither the body nor the mind. The body and mind are the instruments we use. Further, the emotions are temporary. They come and go. They are like flares that shoot into the night sky. They appear for some time and then fade away in the sky of consciousness. But who-we-truly-are is permanent and remains untouched by these flares.

This understanding helps us detach from the emotions and connect with the alert awareness that witnesses them. When we practice meditation to detach from our thoughts, body sensations, and emotions, we begin to become familiar with the constant background of awareness that is witnessing them all.

Being vigilant is essential to remain detached. When we are not alert, the natural tendency is to identify with the stories arising from the injured memories and their associated emotions.

When we resist the emotions that arise with the revival of an injured memory, we energize and strengthen them. When we vigilantly witness them from a detached standpoint, it helps de-energize them, leading to their release.

We need to have an alert awareness that is uncompromisingly focused on itself. It uses emotions and thoughts that arise as hooks to defocus from what arises and focus on our living presence that is observing it all.

To begin with, we may find it difficult to practice this perfectly. It is possible that a certain emotion lasted for ten minutes, but we could watch it only for about two minutes without being affected. Even these two minutes go a long way towards building our spiritual strength.

The practice of detached witnessing can save us from many karmic scars and negative afflictions. We can experience the magic when an event we would otherwise expect to add to our karmic scars passes by without affecting us. These spectacles can make us immune to hurtful emotions.

Let's discuss the cutter and the torch in the next chapter.

15

The Tools For Healing – 2

We discussed the duster of forgiveness and the spectacles of detached witnessing in the last chapter. Now, let us understand the cutter and the torch.

The cutter of Let go

Many people find it difficult to let go of things. Such people build a junkyard around them, always thinking they need every little thing, no matter how useless it is.

The same applies to situations, feelings, and memories. People want to hold on to them, whether they are good or bad, positive or negative. They replay those memories and dwell on those thoughts and feelings, hoping that they can bring them back to life or that something will change.

Be it material things or memories, holding onto anything leads to stagnation. Stagnant water gets infested with germs which can be harmful. Similarly, the feelings and fixations we hold onto stagnate our mind and obstruct the free flow and freshness from our life.

Letting go of whatever we cling to makes room for something new and fresh. Many of us have trouble letting go of the pain from our past. All those painful memories become part of our identity. Many of us do not know who we are without our past pain. This makes it impossible for us to let go of the pain.

No matter how strong and difficult these bondages are, we must learn to use the cutter of Let go.

Releasing meditation

You can practice the Releasing meditation every night before going to bed. It can help you get rid of unwanted thoughts and tendencies that do not serve your progress.

1. Set a timer for ten minutes. Close your eyes and sit in a comfortable posture.

2. Tell yourself, "I will reap the ultimate benefit from this meditation. I wish to get rid of all unwanted thoughts, feelings, and stress. Thank you for this opportunity to empty the unnecessary baggage I have been carrying within me."

3. Remind yourself that even if you let go of everything held within, it doesn't mean you won't get anything. What is truly yours will surely come to you in abundance. What is not meant to be yours will disappear from your life. With this understanding, rest assured that there is nothing to lose and everything to gain.

4. Ask yourself:
    - What are the past impressions I still cling to?

- What are the feelings that haunt me from time to time?
- What are the scenes that I keep avoiding?
- What are the wrong or limiting beliefs that hinder my growth?

5. Dwell in silence for some time for the answers to emerge from within. The answers need not be in words. They can be some past impressions, impulses, or emotions.

6. After listening to the answers, ask yourself, "Is it possible for me to let go of all these?" Tell yourself, "I can break free of all these and lead a blissful life. So, it is safe to let go. What is truly mine will come to me in abundance."

7. Tighten your fist and release it slowly while chanting, "Let go… Let go… Let go…."

8. Ask yourself:
    - Can I permit myself to make mistakes?
    - Can I accept it if things don't work as per my plan?
    - Can I allow myself to be free?
    - Can I let go of the inclinations that bind me?

9. You will surely get an affirmative answer from within. Again, tighten your fist and chant, "Let go… Let go… Let go…" while slowly releasing it.

10. Continue this practice till you reach a state where it no longer matters to you whether anything happens in your life or not. You have let go of your fixations about how life should be or shouldn't be.

11. Check all the hidden needs that you may have harbored. Now, it is time to uncover them. Know all the situations

you wish to escape and the desires you have nurtured to escape them.

12. Tell yourself, "Can I allow myself to release these desires? They do not serve my true purpose. Hence, it is safe to let go of them. I release them fully."

13. Tighten your fist and say, "I am releasing all my hidden desires that no longer serve me." Release your fist slowly and chant, "Let go… Let go… Let go…."

14. Keep chanting "Let go…" for a while until you feel a deep sense of peace and relief.

15. Before ending the meditation, proclaim your freedom and enjoy the beginning of a fresh life by raising your hands and chanting, "I am free… I am freedom!"

16. Keep faith that you have nothing to lose by letting go of whatever is being held within. You are purifying your mind. This will only help in unleashing your highest potential.

17. Finally, when the timer goes off, express gratitude for the opportunity to free yourself and then open your eyes.

Keep using the cutter of Let go every day. Soon, you will begin to experience newfound peace, assurance, cheerfulness, and enthusiasm.

The torch of understanding

In the dark, if we mistake a rope for a snake, we will seek a stick to hit the apparent snake. But we need a torch to see the rope as a rope.

Karmic bondages are created in the unseen. Hence, people cannot see the bondages that burden them and the new ones they create every day. They blame the world for their difficulties and suffering.

The torch of understanding makes it possible to clearly see what we are ailing from and determine the path to freedom. With understanding, we recognize how the world mirrors what lies within us. We correct ourselves within and begin to see changes in the world.

Here, understanding does not mean knowledge of the world. True understanding gives us clarity that helps us to see things beyond the limitations of our individual personality. We get a bird's eye view of how everything works in life. With clarity, we become open to conflicting viewpoints and can see their underlying unity. There is unbiased acceptance of the way things are.

A famous proverb says, "A problem well-stated is half-solved." In other words, understanding the problem is the first and the most important step towards its solution. Therefore, the more we read, the deeper we contemplate, and the better we understand karmic bondages, the better we can use the torch of understanding.

These are the tools available to us to heal our injured memories. By letting go, we accept people and situations just as they are. By seeking forgiveness and forgiving others, we begin to nullify our karmic account. Thus, with forgiveness, we heal; by letting go, we grow. The daily practice of detached witnessing helps us avoid creating new karmic scars with those around us.

In Part 3 of the book, we will discuss the approach to recognize and learn our SOUL lessons.

PART 3

THE LEARNING APPROACH

16

The Benchmark for A Successful Life

Life on Earth is like a school where man has come to learn his SOUL lessons and heal his injured memories. Since most people are unaware of this purpose, they define and pursue worldly yardsticks for measuring success. They acquire and enjoy wealth and comforts; they achieve many milestones in their career or business. Yet, if they do not learn their SOUL lessons, their life is a failure, an opportunity wasted.

Consider a student who has prepared for an English language test. But when he goes to school the next day, he learns that he has a Mathematics exam that day, not English!

What would he end up doing? Throughout the test, he sits in the exam hall, feeling lost. He has no clue what to write as he has not prepared for it. He knows his grammar and vocabulary well, but that would not help him with Algebra or Geometry! He nudges those around him, trying to copy the answers from them. He thinks of ways to distract the supervisor. He is so restless that he ends up making everyone around him just as restless.

Through this example, we are trying to understand how, despite being well-informed, many of us have forgotten and never cared to remember and contemplate our SOUL lessons.

***

The demon king Ravana of the Indian epic the Ramayana, is a classic example of such a student. He ruled the kingdom of Lanka. He amassed immense wealth and earned fame by capturing other kingdoms. But all these achievements were not the measure of his success in Earth-life. He did everything else except learning his SOUL lessons of humility and piety. Being intoxicated by arrogance, he became the icon of wickedness by disturbing the austerities of pious sages and abducting Sita. Thus, he refrained from learning his SOUL lessons and aggravated his karmic bondage. Instead of healing injured memories, he worsened them. His life on Earth ended as a failure.

Adolf Hitler can be considered an example of a student of the twentieth century. His SOUL lesson was to wipe out the karmic scars of cruelty by practicing compassion. But like Ravana, he did just the opposite. He attained the zenith of brutality by causing mass genocide. He ordered the killing of hundreds of thousands of innocent people, thus increasing karmic bondage countless times. We cannot fathom the gravity of the painful and hateful memories created during the Holocaust.

So, we can see how both the characters came to Earth school to learn their SOUL lessons. In the process of learning their lessons of humility and compassion, they would have faced discomfort in overcoming memories of brutality and vengeance planted in them.

But eventually, had they tried to learn their lessons, they would have attained lasting satisfaction.

But as they were unaware of their curriculum, they chose the easy way of furthering their arrogance and brutality aggravating their memories in the process. They wreaked havoc and terror in the lives of those around them in the examination hall of life. Their life ended in failure, having not learned their SOUL lessons.

***

Let us now consider the life of Angulimal, which demonstrates how learning one's SOUL lessons can lead to a complete transformation in one's life. The story is from the time of the Buddha. Angulimal was a forest thug who created panic in the surroundings. He not only robbed the travelers but also cut off their fingers and strung them to his menacing garland as trophies. He used to derive ferocious pleasure by hurting people.

Just like Ravana and Hitler, he was also planted with dangerous memories of vengeance, malice, and cruelty. His life purpose was to heal them, just like the other two.

Once, when the Buddha was traveling through the forest, Angulimal stopped him and stood in his way. He roared, "Take out all your belongings and leave them here. Otherwise, I will kill you. I am the strongest and most feared person here."

The Buddha calmly said, "How can I believe you are the strongest person in this kingdom? You must prove it. Bring some leaves from that tree." Angulimal plucked a few leaves and presented them to the Buddha.

Then the Buddha said, "Now put these leaves back on the tree. If you can't keep something so small back where it was, how can you be the strongest? If you can't create, at least don't destroy. If you cannot give life to someone, you have no right to take their life."

Angulimal realized his mistake after listening to the Buddha's words. He confessed all his crimes to the Buddha and surrendered at his feet. He started following the path shown by the Buddha.

Since Angulimal had committed so many heinous crimes, it was not easy for him to settle his karmic account. Nevertheless, he patiently tolerated abuses, insults, and stone-pelting from the people. He received his karmic paybacks gracefully.

He lived by the teachings of the Buddha and practiced penance and meditation. He sought forgiveness from the bottom of his heart. He felt the gravity of his past cruelty and could empathize with how his victims would have felt. When people pelted stones at him, he would feel compassionate about their plight and say, "Now I can understand the hatred you feel. I can feel your pain." Seeing the blood pouring out of his wounds, he would say, "Let this impure blood go... Let it flow and purify me... It would be the rightful payback." He was prepared to die in retribution for his sins.

Angulimal healed himself by empathizing with those who had suffered his crimes. It was clear to him that he should heal all painful memories by practicing the lessons of empathy, kindness, compassion, and forgiveness. With every passing day, he felt more and more peaceful and contented. Eventually, he healed all his injured memories and became famous for his benevolence.

***

Points to consider: If a vicious and brutal thug like Angulimal, who killed and maimed many people, could absolve himself, heal his memories, and attain purity of mind, then how much more chance do we stand? So, there is no reason to lose hope and every reason to feel heartened and inspired. No matter how many hurtful memories we have, they can all be healed.

The other important point is about the true yardstick to measure success in Earth-life. We are not judging the lives of Ravana,

Hitler, or Angulimal. No one can impose a judgment on anyone's life. In the end, it is we who assess our own Earth-life and decide how we fared. Ultimately, our sense of satisfaction and inner peace determines whether this life was well-lived or there was much left to be desired.

Angulimal was fortunate to be guided by the Buddha due to which he could remember his SOUL purpose. We, too, can consider ourselves fortunate that we are now gaining this understanding of how to make our life worthwhile.

17

The Urgency to Learn Our Lessons

One of the deepest beliefs most of us hold is that the death of our physical body is the end of our existence; when our body perishes, we cease to exist.

This is because we have assumed our physical body as "I," leading to the belief, "I am this body." Due to this strong conditioning, the assumed "I" seems very real.

The belief "I will die" instills deep fear within us. All other fears stem from this fundamental fear. It is a consuming desire to survive in some way. We are unaware of the unnecessary hardships and suffering we endure to ensure the continuity of life as an individual.

The perpetual cycle of bondage and healing

Everyone's journey is unique. The problems each one faces are different. Whether the problems in the external world are resolved or not, it is more important to feel complete from within. Nature inherently leads everyone towards completeness.

Even though we may feel that we have undertaken individual journeys, it is really the journey of the Self. The Self has created all human bodies to derive certain experiences for experiencing completeness. Death of the body does not imply the death of the Self. The Self is beyond both birth and death. Life always continues.

When our injured memories are triggered, the associated bondages are revived. This goes on until the memories are healed, and we feel complete. But in the process, we may also inadvertently create more bondages. The new bondages we create then need to be resolved. This cycle of bondage and healing goes on perpetually.

Without this understanding, we keep feeling unhappy and dissatisfied with our circumstances. Every little incident affects us, and we lose hope. Our fears force us to act in ways that aggravate karmic bondages. And these bondages continue to affect further body-minds due to re-use of their memories.

If we instill this understanding within ourselves, life will become easier to wade through. This does not necessarily mean that the people or situations in our life will change. Rather, this understanding will change our perception of people and situations. They will stop affecting us the way they used to. We will view people with a mature perspective. We will appreciate that we and everyone around us are seeking completeness.

We have pledged to attain completeness, and we must work towards it. But while doing so, we need not worry about the continuity of life. Life goes on eternally. With the surrender of the fear of death comes freedom from all the mistakes we commit while fearing for our lives.

The choice at the "Y" junction in life

The incompleteness within us gives rise to a restless feeling. How we label this restlessness decides how we move further in life. This is the junction where we either choose the path of delusion or absolution. Perceive this point as the "Y" junction.

On the path of delusion lies the fear of death and the aggravation of karmic bondages. On the path of absolution lies the pledge of healing and completeness. Which one do we choose? The torch of understanding helps us choose the right path.

When situations torment, remember that they are due to the feeling of incompleteness because we haven't learned some lessons yet. Contemplate what those lessons are and how to learn them.

Nature makes a specific arrangement around us to help us learn our lessons. Each of us is surrounded by people with various behavioral patterns. Some tend to be angry; some keep instigating us; some don't respect our feelings; and some keep avoiding us. These people are carefully placed around us as contributors to further our learning. Even our behavioral patterns and mindset are a part of this arrangement.

These external and internal factors of the arrangement together give rise to certain situations that hold lessons within them. Every situation brings us a lesson, and if we can grasp it, we automatically feel satisfaction within.

Generally, we choose to deal only with people and situations that we find comfortable. However, by dealing this way, we would return after our Earth-life without learning anything new. We will just brush up on what we already knew.

It will be like a student who only revises lessons he already knows for his exams and skips all the difficult ones. However, the difficult lessons are the most important. Dealing with difficult people and situations is the point of our journey. They are the sources of our lessons leading us to completeness.

We must step out of our comfort zone and face people and situations appropriately, regardless of whether we are comfortable with them or not. Only then can we make way for every lesson to present itself and grasp it. So, prepare to choose well at every "Y" junction in our daily life.

Awareness to learn our lessons

At home, we do not need to be concerned or conscious about how we dress, behave, or move. We are comfortable in a familiar environment. However, when we are outside, we need to be more alert about these things. Hence, we keep higher awareness when we are in unfamiliar surroundings.

The same applies to people and situations too. We find life easier with people who respond or behave the way we want. We feel comfortable with them. We do not have to be highly aware amid them. But with difficult people and situations, we must keep a higher level of awareness. This awareness is necessary for us to learn our lessons.

The grey period

Consider a six-inch scale. The part of the scale between the third and fourth inch represents the part of our life that we *know*, the part that we are aware of.

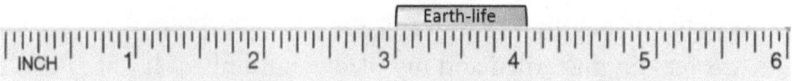

The part before the 3-inch mark and after the 4-inch mark represents what was before Earth-life and what follows Earth-life. These parts of life are unknown to us.

The period shown between the third and fourth inch of the scale, indicates life on Earth. We are unaware of what happened before we embarked on our Earth-life and what will transpire at the end of our earthly existence.

Immediately after the end of our Earth-life, we go through a period of life review known as the grey period. During the grey period, we are elevated to a state of awareness where we can see life in its entirety. We can see all six inches of the scale, all at once. We review how our life on Earth has been.

When we are here on Earth, our view is limited by the individual viewpoint of our body-mind. We treat whatever is inside the skin as "me" and everything else as "other." Hence, our perceptions tend to be biased. But during the grey period, we get a bird's eye view of how we lived our life. We get a viewpoint that is beyond our body-mind. We empathize with the people who were around us. We clearly see those aspects that were unknown to us when we made certain choices on Earth.

Based on this higher perspective, we judge the film of our life. We intuitively realize the lessons we had pledged to learn. We pat our backs for those lessons we did learn. But we also see how we avoided or refused to learn certain key lessons.

Those who regret their choices and the time that was squandered away during their Earth-life surmise, "I never did what I had descended to the Earth for. I was given the perfect opportunity. The arrangement was ideal too. I had the right people around me who were co-creating situations to fulfill my purpose. And yet, my lessons remain unlearned and my pledge unfulfilled. If only I could realize this, then. Why couldn't I understand then that what I was doing was not what I was *supposed* to do?"

Let us try to answer this question.

Be a seeker of truth, not a judge

We fail to realize that our responses are not aligned with our purpose because we live like a *judge* during our Earth-life. And later, when we look back at our life during the grey period, we become a *seeker of truth*.

We should do the exact opposite. We should be a seeker of truth during our Earth-life and our own judge during the grey period. For this, we need to train ourselves.

When someone shouts or abuses us, we act as a judge and label him as reckless. We retort angrily. However, if we are a seeker of truth, we would not judge them based on their words or actions.

A seeker of truth would contemplate, not retaliate. We would understand that, just like us, the other person also has some unresolved memories that seek healing and completion. He is acting helplessly to find completeness. This realization would make us respond peacefully with maturity. We would place ourselves in his shoes and try to understand why he could be behaving the way he does.

In the process, we will also learn our SOUL lessons that the situation is trying to teach us. Patience, calmness, understanding, and empathy are some lessons the situation could hold for us.

Later, during the grey period, when we look back at the same incident, we can fully empathize with what the other person was feeling at that juncture. We are elevated to a state of awareness where we not only look back at every incident of our life from a top view but also perceive how others felt due to our responses. Thus, we act as a seeker of truth during the grey period. We contemplate and regret why we reacted angrily when the other person needed our empathy. However, it would be too late then to mend matters. It doesn't help to be a seeker of truth in the grey period.

We can judge any movie only after watching it completely. Similarly, we can judge our choices and actions after reviewing our life from start to end during the grey period. After watching the entire life film, we can evaluate our time on Earth. Was our lifetime successful or a failure? Is there any unfinished business? That is the time to become our judge.

While living on Earth, we constantly judge ourselves and others. We label events and people as good or bad. These judgments are often proved wrong as they are based on our preconceived notions. Once we move on to the astral plane, our perspectives change completely, and we can assess our lifetime without biases.

Hence, our goal should be to achieve the seeker-state of the grey period during Earth-life itself. If we could be a seeker instead of a judge here, we would be able to contemplate how others are affected by our thoughts, feelings, words, and actions before it is too late. We would also be alert enough to learn our lessons from situations. By being judgmental and knowing only our side of the story, we neither help others nor ourselves attain completeness.

Take the quantum leap

When we look back at our life, we feel guilty if we were not empathetic towards others. We also feel guilty for not learning our lessons when we were provided with the perfect setting. This guilt becomes an injured memory. We transition from the grey period into the afterlife with this injured memory.

The memories we hold during this transition determine the plane of consciousness we naturally move towards. If we learn our SOUL lessons, we transition to the afterlife with a feeling of completeness.

We are all bearing injured memories that need healing. They could be over fifty, a hundred, or even a thousand years' worth. Everyone is carrying a different quantity. Each one's stock of memories varies, and it is not clear to us how much we carry. We can only do our best to understand this topic and start healing them. This means we are trying to take a quantum leap by accomplishing the work of many years in a very short period.

It could take thirty, forty, or even fifty years to get there, but we all get there eventually if we persevere. No matter how long it takes, it is important that we get to spend the rest of our lives on Earth in a *healed and blissful state.*

Since we are trying to take this quantum leap, we must deeply understand this subject, reflect on it, and make it a part of our daily practice with a sense of urgency. We are reading the theory in this book to practice it in everyday life.

With a sense of urgency, start contemplating the people and situations around us. Understand who they really are and why they exist in our life. What are they trying to teach us, and what do they need from us? This should become a daily practice.

Learnings from Near Death Experiences

Some people have encountered what is popularly known as Near Death Experience (NDE). When faced with life-threatening events, like accidents or terminal illness, they experienced being temporarily outside their physical body. Doctors pronounced them dead.

Most of the NDE narratives share a common theme that describes people hovering outside their body and being led through a long whirling tunnel towards a source of light that they could see at the end of the tunnel. The light became brighter but more pleasant and soothing as they passed through the tunnel. Some of them had flashes of insight during this period.

When they eventually returned into their physical body, their perspective of life was transformed. It was as if they were looking at life from a higher dimension, which changed their choices and values.

What did they learn during the NDE? Many remembered the forgotten facets of their life, which was life-transforming for them. It completely changed how they related to people and their approach to their life's endeavors. A common observation was that they broke free of the fear of death because they could experience being alive even after leaving their body.

Most of them testified how their entire Earth-life flashed before them. They could see how their life was spent - being tensed about trivial things, complaining over things that didn't matter in the final equation. Many of them saw the utter futility of what they pursued in their life. They realized they hadn't effectively used the opportunity that Earth-life offered them.

On returning, they were grateful to live every single day, being given a chance to make amends and live a truly worthwhile life. Their interests changed from the mundane and materialistic to the profound and spiritual. All because of the flash of insight that their NDE offered them.

However, we need not wait for an NDE to gain the same insight! We can achieve the same paradigm shifts through deep contemplation to re-assess our life priorities and purpose.

18

Heeding The Voice of Conscience

We have seen how people and situations are tailor-made arrangements made by nature to help us learn our SOUL lessons. This arrangement is an expression of nature's benevolence.

While people and situations are external arrangements, some arrangements are also made within us. The Self continuously guides us from within through our feelings and intuition. Here, intuition means the wise voice of conscience.

The voice of conscience indicates when we fall out of alignment with the free flow of nature. It nudges us through a bad feeling as if to say, "You're not thinking in line with what God wants from you," or "What you're doing does not serve your life's purpose." This feedback is constantly provided to us.

The more we heed the wise voice of our conscience, the clearer it can be felt. When people stop heeding their wise voice, they start indulging in wrongdoings. Their wise voice becomes muted.

For example, when Rita gained knowledge about the SOUL purpose and the need to learn her lessons, she decided to work on the lesson of self-control. She resolved to abstain from feeling, thinking, or speaking bitter and hurtful words to others. She made up her mind that she would only bless others. She remained vigilant during the first week of her resolution.

One morning, her neighbor knocked at her door. As soon as Rita opened the door, the neighbor, visibly outraged, screamed at her, "Don't you realize that the muddy water from your balcony is dirtying my windowpanes? I've told you umpteen times to place plates under your potted plants. You just don't understand."

Rita got livid and retorted, "If you're so troubled by a few drops of water, go and stay in a mansion where no one will disturb you."

Her inner voice kept reminding her, "Forgive her. There's no need to react angrily. Calm down. Control your words." But she didn't heed her conscience and continued shouting. As she was not attuned to her inner voice, she entirely forgot about her resolution of self-control.

Nature created an ideal situation for Rita to practice self-control. Her wise voice also reminded her. But as the noise of anger dominated her wise voice, she couldn't stick to her resolution.

This is how we neglect our wise voice of intuition. When we are served spicy, deep-fried, or sugary food, our wise voice keeps reminding us that excessive indulgence in such food can harm our health. But we fall for the lure of our taste buds and neglect it.

When we deceive someone or speak arrogantly, our wise voice nudges us, "You're going wrong," but we suppress it. Gradually the wise voice gets muted and stops guiding us. Without the compass of our wise voice, we unknowingly lose our way in life. We create complications and spend our life in trying to resolve them.

Let us understand this with an analogy.

There are two siblings in a family. The elder son has a loud voice. He shouts, screams, and repeatedly persuades his mother to satisfy his whims. Their mother listens to him and fulfills all his wishes. The younger son speaks in a feeble voice and keeps silent after saying anything just once. He does not insist that his mother should do his bidding. He dwells in peace after stating his wish.

Here the elder son represents the noise of the mind, while the younger son symbolizes the voice of conscience – the guidance of the Self. Listening to this voice is crucial as it intuitively leads us to our SOUL lessons.

The loud noise is the pull of sensory attractions, while the wise voice is the call of our SOUL lessons. People get so engrossed in the glitzy world of sensory allures that they keep listening to its loud noise and neglect the wise voice. They are lost in the pursuit of pleasing their senses to such an extent that their wise voice gradually gets dimmed and finally muted. They stop getting guidance from their conscience.

Suppose two songs are being played simultaneously – one is loud, and the other is hardly audible. If your attention is not well-trained, you will hear only the loud song. But when you practice focusing on subtle sounds, you can catch even the song played at a low volume.

A mother is receptive to her child's voice. When he plays outside the house, she can still hear his cries and reach him. Similarly, you need to increase your attunement with the divine guidance provided by your intuition.

Develop receptivity to intuition

Here are some steps to develop your intuition for learning your SOUL lessons.

1. Recognize when the message is being communicated

Intuitions are transmitted continuously. If grasped well, they can tell us exactly what needs to be done at any moment. These messages can be anything from a spoken word, a signboard, a book we read, or the words of a song we hear.

Communication from within can often be very subtle, like a feeling, hunch, or fleeting image. Guidance can also come from physical sensations like uneasiness in the stomach, goosebumps, or a sense of sudden relief.

Sometimes if the messages seem too obscure, we can mentally seek a clearer guidance from our heart. In this way, we can attune ourselves to receive the messages from our intuition.

2. Seeking specific guidance

If you are looking for guidance on a particular situation or dilemma, you can mentally ask specific questions to receive answers from within. But having sought inner guidance, it is equally important to get into the receiving mode for the answers. This is where meditation plays an important role.

3. Practice meditation

Regular meditation helps us detach from the incessant noise of thoughts in the head and shift to the serenity of the heart. Spending 10 to 15 minutes at the same time every day can deepen our attunement with the heart and recognize when our intuition speaks.

4. Writing down the answers

Messages arising from our intuition are subtle and can fade out of our awareness within seconds. Hence, it helps to write down the insights that arise as quickly as possible, lest they are lost. When we write down these flashes of insight, we are indicating to nature that we are open to receive guidance and serious about acting on them.

We can maintain a journal for recording intuitions for ten minutes every day. This practice is a way of strengthening the power of intuition. When this is consistently practiced, we will marvel at the clarity of what comes through from the heart. Our decisions will arise from the wise voice, which cannot be matched by any level of rationale or analytical reasoning.

5. Take prompt action

When we act sincerely and promptly on the inner guidance, we begin to receive even more guidance that is specific and easier to decipher. Faith is the key to action. When we trust our intuition and act, we begin to harmonize and synchronize our life with higher guidance.

19

Recognizing Your SOUL Lessons

A boy joined a martial arts school to learn karate. The instructor evaluated him by asking him to mimic some of the moves. He told the boy, "We will have to tie your right hand during the initial weeks of training. You will have to practice all the moves with your left hand."

The boy was baffled. He wondered why he should be restricted in this manner, given that he was adept at using his right hand. Seeing the puzzled look on the boy's face, his uncle, who had accompanied him for enrolment, complained, "What a torture this is on my nephew! Others are fighting with both hands. Why should he be made to struggle with one hand?"

The instructor explained, "His left hand is weak and rigid because he seldom uses it. I noticed that he uses his right hand more to compensate for his left. All his limbs are flexible, except for his left hand. To improve its flexibility and strengthen it, we will restrict the use of his right hand."

The boy agreed and started training the same day. Although he kept failing and was beaten several times, he kept practicing with his left hand. Eventually, his left hand developed strength and became agile and flexible. Then the instructor asked him to let loose his right hand and fight. That day, he proved to be unbeatable!

Identify the "left hand" in your life

We also need to identify *our* left hand to practice in the school of Earth-life. Which habit or belief makes us rigid? Which tendency becomes our weakness? Everyone's "left hand" is different. Nature makes special arrangements to make it strong and flexible.

The example of the boy, who wanted to learn karate, is easy to understand because his left and right hands are tangible. But identifying and understanding our SOUL lessons is not as straightforward because they are intangible. We have to introspect and seek them within us.

We need to reflect on those aspects of our life where we lack flexibility. For instance, if we lack patience, then patience is our left hand. Nature arranges for us to develop patience. Similarly, if we lack courage or confidence, then these are our left hands. Situations will be scripted in our life that evoke fear or timidity so that we get the opportunity to develop courage and confidence.

The boy's right hand was tied to create opportunities to flex his left hand. When we play the board game of carrom, we shoot the coins by placing the striker within the bounds of the two lines. This challenges us to develop our shooting skills. If we are allowed the freedom to place the striker anywhere on the board, we can never develop our game skills.

Likewise, we, too, are bound by limitations that challenge us to unleash our latent qualities. Limitations teach us patience, perseverance, and resilience to step out of our comfort zone.

But how do we identify our left hand? How do we recognize our SOUL lessons? We will consider four lenses (determining factors) that can help us know our lessons.

1. Repeating events and situations

Nature is constantly working on us. It keeps casting baited fishhooks to weed out our karmic scars. The fishhooks, in this case, are people, events, or situations that revive our injured memories and trigger the associated emotions. They are the paybacks sent by nature from our karmic account in the hope that we will get rid of the karmic bondage by receiving them gracefully.

However, when we are unaware of nature's providence, we unhook ourselves and let go of the opportunity. We either escape our lessons or react in ways that create new scars instead of healing old ones.

But nature never gives up on us! It keeps repeating similar incidents until we learn the lesson that was baited on nature's fishhook. Thus, repeating events or situations are a powerful lens to identify our lessons.

If we often find ourselves in the company of intimidating people or situations that trigger fear within us, courage is our lesson. Faith could be our lesson if we often feel let down by people who break our trust. If we keep falling short of fulfilling our commitments, we may need to develop trustworthiness. Focus and perseverance are our SOUL lessons if we keep getting distracted and sidetracked from our goals.

2. The world mirror

The world is not as it appears to us; the world is how *we are*.

Understanding this important principle can help us heal our memories and transform our life.

Our world is a screen upon which we project our mental traits and unresolved memories. It reflects what we hold within us.

Let us understand how the world mirrors us. If we consistently experience that people are unhelpful and non-cooperative, it could mean that, in some ways, we are not helping ourselves or others. Perhaps, cooperation and generosity are our key lessons. If we find that people do not take us seriously and ignore us, they could be reflecting our own lack of self-belief and self-worth. Developing self-belief could possibly be our SOUL lesson. If the people around us are disorganized, they may be mirroring the chaotic and disorganized state of our own thoughts and priorities. Perhaps, focus and discipline could be our lesson.

To begin with, it may seem somewhat farfetched that the world reflects our mind. But when we experiment with this principle, we will be convinced how true this is. We get lost in the details of the world, due to which we do not realize that these details are only living pictures of what lies buried within our mind.

Thus, we can use the way the world appears to us as a lens to determine our shortcomings and the corresponding SOUL lessons.

3. Our limiting beliefs

No incident or situation is a problem in itself. It becomes a so-called problem or triggers blame or complaint within us only because we are viewing it through the filter of our limiting beliefs.

A belief is like a roof supported by the pillars of evidence. Without evidence, beliefs collapse. The more evidence we get, the stronger our beliefs become. And the stronger our beliefs, the more evidence we get. Given enough time, the roof of belief becomes so strong that it no longer needs the pillars of evidence. It stands on its own. In effect, the belief becomes our indisputable truth.

The beliefs we hold within us create an illusory reality, which we assume as our truth. This illusory reality distorts our self-image, and we begin to define ourselves based on this distorted self-image.

When we are caught up in a poor self-image, we get limited by beliefs like "I don't deserve," "I'm not worthy," "I am not enough," "I am not lovable," "Things come hard in my life," or "I can't trust people." These limiting beliefs could be either inherited through our injured memories or from our childhood conditioning.

Loving acceptance is the key to transcending the limiting beliefs that resonate in our world. To release the beliefs that are held within, bring them to light first and accept them completely. Heal all such deep-seated impressions through the practice of forgiveness.

Daily introspection can reveal our limiting beliefs. Once we identify our limiting beliefs, we can replace them with new positive thoughts, which align with love, joy, peace, and harmony.

4. Our escapism

Our tendency to escape uncomfortable feelings clearly indicates where our lessons lie. For this, we need to develop a witness mindset. We must witness the play of emotions that compel us to act or react in fixed ways.

We need to catch ourselves when we try to avoid certain people or situations by diverting our attention to something more pleasurable. Perhaps we choose to watch TV, go shopping, or keep binging on food. These are getaways our subconscious mind naturally pursues to dodge pain and discomfort.

While courage and patience are lessons in themselves, they help us confront our fears and impulses to learn other SOUL lessons.

We have discussed the lenses that can help us recognize our unfinished business in Earth-life and identify our SOUL lessons. In the next chapter, we shall discuss the mindset required to learn our lessons.

20

The Learning Mindset

We generally classify people into two contrasting groups – the weak and the strong, the successful and the failures, or the competent and the incompetent. However, none of that matters for developing the mindset required for learning our SOUL lessons. What matters is whether we are learners or non-learners.

Those who do not believe in continuous learning try to survive on their existing abilities, skills, and track record. They are bent on proving themselves based on what they have achieved rather than what they could potentially be. They constantly judge and brand themselves and others because they believe in fixed capabilities.

Conversely, those willing to constantly learn and work on themselves always focus on possibilities. For them, their existing capabilities are only a milestone. They believe that new skills and abilities can be cultivated with an open mind through focused effort. They do not bother to judge because they believe everyone can change and develop themselves.

With a learning mindset, they won't waste time proving how good they are when they can be better. They won't hide their weaknesses when they can overcome them and develop new strengths. They won't seek appreciation from others when they can seek motivation from those who challenge them.

Given a choice between re-trying an easy puzzle you've already solved and trying a new-but-difficult puzzle, what will you choose?

Non-learners stick to already tried and safe things. They prefer to do what they are already good at rather than take up difficult challenges. Learners love new challenges. They are ready to fail because failure is only a stepping-stone for them.

Attitude towards failure

How we perceive failure determines our ability to learn our SOUL lessons. We can consider ourselves a failure only when we get disheartened by setbacks and stop learning. Otherwise, failure is just another name for a stepping-stone. It is a springboard to leap higher.

Looking back on our choices made five years ago, we may find a few decisions absurd or senseless now. Does that mean we failed? Not at all! All our past decisions were based on our knowledge and understanding at that time. It only means that we are growing; we have become wiser.

If we just live in a comfort zone where we refrain from going wrong, we can never unleash our true potential. No need to get discouraged or give up simply because we made the wrong choices. Instead, do the best every time because our persistent practice can propel the learning process of our SOUL lessons.

Set aside time to regularly reflect on the challenges life has presented, the ones we have bypassed, our honest reasons for avoiding them, and what we can do next to learn our lessons.

The role of contemplation in learning

In the earlier chapter, we saw how we assess our life film during the grey period after transitioning from Earth-life. We evaluate how successful we were in fostering relationships and gaining skills to make the mind steadfast, obedient, pure, and loving.

But we need not wait for the grey period for such contemplation. Nature presents us this opportunity and ample time to make corrections even during Earth-life. We can regard this time as a Grace period! It can be at the end of the year before the dawn of the next, even between two events, two days. It can also be between the end of one project and the start of the next.

During this period, we can contemplate: What lessons did we learn? What did we do well? Did we meet the targeted goals? What learning opportunities did we miss? What mistakes did we commit? How will we overcome them next time? What are the 20% aspects that we can work upon within ourselves that will bring 80% change in the quality of our life?

Non-learners do not bother to assess their lives and decide on course corrections. They fail to decode the messages nature provides them.

Without contemplation, diamonds remain mere pieces of coal. Well-directed contemplation plays a pivotal and decisive role in leading us to our SOUL lessons. It is the process of gleaning through our experiences to unearth the hidden lessons we are meant to learn.

Let's discuss some key aspects that can help us with our contemplation.

1. Action is inseparable from contemplation

Contemplation is incomplete without action. Action is blind without contemplation. Contemplation is not just about thinking. It should be followed by action. When we gain a thorough understanding through contemplation, our thoughts automatically begin to shape our actions.

2. Consistent introspection

Regular introspection is extremely important. We must reflect again and again to avoid repeating the same mistakes. It will help us cross the threshold to progress further. With consistent introspection, we can become aware of our habitual mistakes and determine not to repeat them.

3. Honest meditation

With contemplation, we realize that we know too little about ourselves. Hence, we must honestly meditate on our thought processes, behavioral patterns, and responses.

Very often, the obvious reasons that we give ourselves for our actions are not the real reasons. We give excuses disguised as "good reasons." Our deep need to be right and perfect compels us to hide our shortcomings. We fear acknowledging our weaknesses, even to ourselves.

Contemplation demands us to honestly tell ourselves the truth about how and why we think and feel in certain ways. Only then can we see through the layers of our conditioning and injured memories to unearth our lessons.

Honest meditation is an effective way of throwing light on the dark corners of our mind. We can make tremendous progress only when we grasp the unseen truth about ourselves. Otherwise, if we continue doing what we have done so far, we won't progress towards our SOUL purpose.

4. Make contemplation a driving force for learning and transformation

Ask yourself the following three questions:

1. What will I gain through contemplation?

If we are unaware of the benefits of contemplation, we won't be motivated enough to begin. Hence, before we begin, we must write down answers to "What will I gain through contemplation?" The answers will lend urgency and genuineness to our contemplation.

2. Do I really want what I can gain through contemplation?

Very often, our words don't align with our actions. We may say, "I want to progress. I want to attain peace and completeness." But when the time comes, we may find that we are not prepared to act on it.

Hence, we need to introspect whether we truly yearn for the benefits arising from our contemplation. The answer should not be merely in words. It should arise from our heart, our innermost core. If we do not get the impetus from the heart, then we must re-visit the first question.

3. Am I prepared to make the changes my contemplation might suggest?

This question is linked to the second one. If we have successfully answered the second question, the answer to the third will be in the affirmative. The third question propels us to action.

Learning why and how to contemplate is of no use unless it is put into practice. Practice is far more important than mere theoretical learning.

When we practice something, learning is implicit in it. But when we learn something theoretically, it does not amount to practicing it. Learning something at the intellectual level can make us get into a lull of complacency that we know the subject or that we are making progress. But real progress can happen only with practice. We develop confidence and gain conviction only with practice.

For example, we can learn about gym exercises and weight-training techniques by watching videos and reading books. But the only way to really build strength is to practice in the gym and lift weights consistently.

Let us now understand some key qualities that can help us learn our other SOUL lessons. These qualities are also SOUL lessons in their own right.

1. Patience

Patience is one of the fundamental qualities required to be a good learner. When we are impatient and impulsive, we often jump to conclusions and create complications in our life. We do not pause to reflect and refine our perspective.

With patience, we learn to wait for life to unfold. We become seers, not doers. Instead of struggling to make things happen, we learn to stand back and allow things to happen. Our chances of learning our lessons improve when we go slow and absorb and assimilate what life is trying to teach us.

2. Detachment and Playfulness

When painful memories are evoked, life can become difficult and depressing. Many of us experience despair when things don't seem to work as we wish. Our daily experiences may even sap our energy, leaving us with little hope or power to shift into a positive mindset.

Nevertheless, we must work through the clouds of negativity that block the sunlight of hope. This is where understanding who-we-truly-are helps us distance ourselves from our thoughts and emotions, no matter how intensely overwhelming they may be.

The practice of meditation helps us detach ourselves from painful sensations, consuming thoughts, and negative emotions. Once we distance ourselves, we achieve half the victory. When we become adept at detaching ourselves, we gradually develop the attitude of playfulness.

Being able to perceive life as a game, with its ups and downs, its highs and lows, helps us detach from the happenings. Partaking in the game of life playfully helps us reclaim ourselves instead of slipping into a victim mindset.

3. Resilience and Persistence

The ability to bounce back from setbacks is a key to the learning process in Earth-life. Having a never-say-die attitude helps us duck the bouncers bowled at us in the game of life.

A famous saying epitomizes resilience: Don't tell God how grave your problems are; instead, tell your problems how great God is!

When we have faith in the divine plan of our life on Earth, we will not quiver in the face of stumbling blocks. We will continue to persevere through the challenges with persistent effort.

4. Wise Sensitivity

Sensitivity is one of the SOUL lessons many of us are here to learn. Being sensitive is essential for empathizing and deeply understanding ourselves and the people around us. Our learning can become subtler when we become sensitive towards our daily situations.

However, mere sensitivity can prove harmful. If we are extremely sensitive to the negative emotions of people we care for, we can soak ourselves with their emotions like a blotting paper. We won't be able to do them any good with such a vulnerable sensitivity.

Sensitivity should be supported by wise discernment. They are the two wings that help us fly. If even one is missing, we cannot rise higher. We should be able to discern the truth and detach ourselves to use our sensitivity for learning our lessons effectively.

5. Devotedness to the SOUL Purpose

A seed needs to sacrifice itself for a sapling to sprout. It should allow its walls to dissolve and merge into the surrounding soil to give way to the sapling. The purpose of the seed is fulfilled only through its sacrifice and willingness to surrender itself for transformation.

So, it is with us. We need to commit ourselves willingly to our SOUL purpose. How intensely do we yearn for completeness? Is it lukewarm, or has it reached the melting point? The ultimate determinant in this journey of learning is the strength of our commitment to fulfilling our SOUL purpose.

The next part of the book offers a deep dive into the major SOUL lessons.

PART 4

A DEEP DIVE INTO OUR SOUL LESSONS

21

The Lesson of Patience

The lesson of patience is part of everyone's curriculum. It is a virtue that can only be understood here on Earth. It is the fundamental lesson required for learning every other SOUL lesson.

An extended trait of patience is tolerance. With tolerance, one patiently goes through painful or unpleasant situations with poise and positive intent, without lamenting.

When we get used to an easy and comfortable way of life, we find it difficult to tolerate even a little discomfort or inconvenience and resist it.

For example, after working from home for many months, when you are suddenly asked to work from the office, you need to travel on traffic-jammed roads and work late. You will find yourself becoming intolerant and angry over petty matters at home and in the office.

The root cause of intolerance is inflexibility and lack of patience. Waiting is agonizing and boring for most people. They aren't aware of the wonder that is set into motion when they abide in the stillness of patience. They not only miss out on the joy of the moment but also often ruin things by trying to force things to happen too quickly. In their haste, they either give the right responses at the wrong time or the wrong responses at the right time. This causes complications. The problem that was about to be solved remains unsolved.

For instance, if you are arguing with your spouse, you may choose the wrong response or timing due to lack of patience. The argument can settle if you learn the art of waiting and responding with measured words at the right time. You just need to restrain yourself; be patient and respond when your emotions are under control. Then your words and actions will be based on love and not hate.

In today's increasingly fast-paced world, most people go about in a frenzy, as if they are blindly running some race. They feel an uncontrollable urge to keep checking their social media apps for content feeds. Without the patience to wait to watch the next episode of a TV serial, they indulge in binge watching. This is becoming an increasingly prevalent culture. Everyone unknowingly starts emulating such behavior by observing others.

It is said that good things come to those who wait. Saint Kabir has beautifully explained the need for patience in his famous couplet.

Dheere dheere re manaa,
Dheere dheere sab kuch hoye.
Maali seenche sau ghadaa,
Rutu aaye fal hoye.

***

O mind, be patient; everything takes its time.
The gardener may pour a hundred pots of water.
But the tree bears fruit only when the season is right.

When you sow the seed of black bamboo, you need to patiently tend to it for several months before the seed sprouts. But once it sprouts, it grows to the height of twenty feet in no time.

Whenever you need to show great patience, remember the black bamboo example. Wait long enough, and you will be rewarded for your patience with astonishing results. All you need to do is take inspired action with patience and persistence.

Everything valuable in life never comes instantly. Whatever we aspire to be in life, we must be patient while learning and practicing it. No skill can be acquired overnight; it takes time. Relationships are also nurtured over time. It takes time to develop trust.

For example, a newlywed girl finds her in-laws' family customs, lifestyle, and values too different for her taste. She will invite trouble if she reacts to them impulsively. She needs to harbor patience and tolerance for some period and learn the ways of the new family. Then she can reap the fruit of a harmonious relationship.

The same applies to her in-laws too. They will only breed disharmony if they expect her to align with their family ways from Day-one. They need to welcome and induct her with love and patience.

We may even have to face failures and get better at persevering with patience to achieve lasting success. To become successful, we must set goals, decide on an action plan, and be patient.

To be happy in every situation, we must patiently practice being happy through the highs and lows of daily life. Gradually we will perfect the art of being happy all the time.

The nature of life on Earth is designed to slow down the manifestation of results. It takes time to implement an idea and see it evolve and crystallize before our eyes. This slow-down in the manifestation helps us to pause and patiently review our choices to arrive at better choices. That is why it is said that even Gods strive for the opportunity to be born as humans.

In the ancient Puranas, Gods are depicted as being impulsive and impatient. There are stories of how they often get caught up in the heat of the moment and utter curses or get trapped in their own words. Being celestial beings does not make them immune to such flaws. For this reason, they are said to seek human birth.

Challenges that contribute to this lesson

Consider patience and tolerance as your lesson if you experience any of the following challenges in your everyday life.

- You feel uncomfortable or restless when you have to wait for people or things to happen.
- You overreact to uncomfortable sensations, scenes, or people who seem difficult.
- You lose your temper and say things that you regret later.
- You don't feel in control of your time and are always in a hurry to catch the time.
- Whether trivial matters or important decisions, you feel the urge to take shortcuts that often backfire.
- You often face situations where people either delay you or your tasks.

Patience transforms a reactive way of living into a creative experience

For many people, the words "act" and "react" are more appealing than "wait." We are so used to always *doing something* that we find it difficult to simply *be*. We believe that doing something is the only way to achieve anything.

Most people lead life by reacting to circumstances based on their past conditioning. Reactive living does not need awareness. It is like following the same beaten path every day. However, if you choose a new unknown path, you need to be aware and patient. Creative living requires you to pause and choose your responses with awareness.

Human evolution is all about moving from reactive living to creative living. When you develop patience and learn to slow down, you open yourself to new ideas and insights. You begin to act less impulsively. Your actions become increasingly intuitive and creative.

Whenever you feel the need to act impulsively, pause and focus on your breath. Watching your breath is the best way to detach from the flurry of thoughts and calm down.

When a music composer creates a piece of music, he introduces pauses between the notes. He intuitively senses how long to wait before playing the next note. The pause between each note lends rhythm and depth to the music. His intuitive waiting brings harmony to the composition.

Similarly, life falls into a beautiful rhythm when we become experts at waiting for the right duration and taking action at the right time.

Tips to learn patience

1. Delayed gratification

Delayed gratification is about deliberately waiting for some time before fulfilling any desire. For instance, wait for some time before answering the phone, posting a message, or playing a mobile game. This does not mean you should stop using the phone; Instead, delay its use for some time.

We are born in the era of click-to-order technology with the specific purpose of developing patience. We want instant results, be it food delivery or sightseeing.

If you feel the urge to order something, ask yourself, "Is this a need or a want? If it is a want, have I fulfilled all my needs?" This will prevent you from making hasty purchases of things you don't really need.

Practice delayed gratification in daily situations to nurture it. For instance, purposely wait for some time before eating your meal. Let your phone ring three to four times before answering it. Similarly, wait for a while before checking your messages or watching videos.

2. Practice thinking before you speak

Many of us tend to speak as we think. At times we blurt out the first thought that comes into our heads without considering the consequences. Practice patience; pause and go over what you want to say. With this, you can avoid hurting or offending others.

3. People around us act as speed-breakers

When we want certain fixed outcomes fast, we hurry things up. But nature knows better than to just give us what we want. So, nature applies brakes to our momentum through the people around us. Their actions and words slow us down, but that drop in momentum is necessary to save us from accidents or goof-ups. Without these brakes, it is quite possible that instead of healing the memories we already had, we end up creating new ones.

Whenever we get annoyed with people for their slow responses or for delaying our tasks, remember that they are only acting as speed-breakers to help us learn the precious quality of patience.

4. Slow down

If you tend to hurry things up, take a deliberate pause. If you want things done immediately and can't wait for things to take their natural course, stop. Being impatient won't make things move fast. Take several deep breaths before you act or make a move. For example, if you're in a long queue at the payment counter of a grocery store or stuck in heavy traffic, take a pause instead of getting worked up. Observe your breath, pray, listen to music, or accept and enjoy the way things are.

5. Make patience your goal for an entire day

Decide a day when you will work on your patience. Make a determined effort to think about everything you do. Be mindful about how you respond to events. At the end of the day, observe how being mindful has helped you make better decisions and get along with people better.

22

The Lesson of Unconditional Love

While some people find it natural and easy to express love spontaneously, some find it difficult and uncomfortable. Instead of feeling love from the heart, they try to think about how it should be.

Feeling loved or being able to express love helps us align with our true nature. Hence, it is the most vital lesson of the human journey.

However, injured memories cause us to shut our heart and feel numb. Bitter or hateful experiences take a toll on the free flow of love from within us. We find it difficult to trust and empathize with others. The experience of love gets choked in our life.

True love is unconditional

Most of us naturally regard unpleasant emotions like anger, hatred, or ill-will as negative feelings. But we assume attachment, disguised as love, to be a positive virtue. Some even consider the feelings of jealousy or possessiveness between two people as love.

However, true love is beyond the personalized love that two or more individuals claim for each other. It is not attachment, attraction, craving, or infatuation. Personalized love may seem selfless but is rooted in attachment to desires.

The experience of true love is independent of how others treat us. It hinges on the love *we* exude and the warmth *we* radiate in any relationship, be it husband-wife, parent-child, siblings, friends, neighbors, or colleagues.

We have been raised in a belief system of conditional love. We have been made to believe that love must be earned. We can find love only when we live up to people's expectations. If we are not good enough, we will be deprived of love. If someone does not love us back, they don't deserve our love.

These beliefs have influenced the collective psyche of families, groups, communities, and societies for generations to such an extent that love has been reduced to fear of denial.

Challenges contributing to this lesson

When a dog chews a bone, its gums bleed. But the dog believes it to be an enjoyable experience and relishes its own blood despite the pain.

Similarly, when we feel hatred and neglect from others, we hold grudges. We find temporary relief when we curse others. But we create karmic scars instead of healing our injured memories. We unknowingly attract more bitterness into our life, multiplied many times over. Nature sends us paybacks in the form of testing situations.

When this goes on for a long time, it eventually affects our physical and mental health. Chronic ailments like diabetes, hypertension, disorders of the heart, thyroid, or kidney set in. We feel disconnected from the world. Mental loneliness creeps in even though we may be in the physical company of people.

We need to treat these symptoms as a wake-up call to let go of our grudges and learn the lesson of unconditional love.

Embracing love

How do we break free from this vicious cycle of hatred? How do we nullify the seeds of bitterness we have already planted in the past?

By choosing to unconditionally love all those for whom we harbor negative feelings. By using the duster of forgiveness, we forgive and seek to be forgiven. By using the cutter of Let go, we release our grudges.

Our hurt feelings pertaining to love exist due to ignorance of our true nature. To learn the lesson of true love, let us dispel our wrong beliefs about love and make certain choices.

1. True love can be experienced only by giving, not by receiving

It is a mass belief that we can have something only when we *receive* it. The same applies to love too. We believe that we can experience love only when we receive it. Hence, we not only expect people to love us but also fix how they should love us. This leads to disappointment.

The experience of true love is not in receiving it but rather in giving it unconditionally. If you receive love, it is merely a bonus.

When a bucket is filled with water to the brim, it overflows. It feels great to expect nothing in return! Similarly, when we are filled with love, we give boundlessly.

Without knowing this, people spend their life waiting for people to shower them with love. Due to this fallacy, they yearn for appreciation, consideration, and approval from people.

For example, someone, who has worked hard all his work life and has never been appreciated, breaks down into tears when his colleagues praise him at his farewell event. He has waited for years to hear a few words of praise or approval. As he is unaware of the power of true love, he seeks it in the external world.

We can never find true and everlasting love in the external world. When injured memories get triggered, they make us feel deprived of love. At such times, we need to remind ourselves: **True love can be experienced only by giving, not by receiving. People who exist in our life are not here to love us. They are here to remind us that we are the source of love.**

Ask yourself: "Why do I need an agent to love myself?" Waiting for the world to love us is like hiring an agent to love us!

It is time to honor ourselves as the source of love. We have undertaken the human journey to realize and express unconditional love. If we truly love ourselves, we won't hurt ourselves by indulging in negative emotions.

When we learn to truly love and forgive ourselves, the nectar of love begins to fill our hearts. When it overflows, it begins to radiate to everyone around us unconditionally.

2. Move beyond the personalized form of love

Many become enamored by people's physical appearances and get attached to their temporary attributes. They live under the illusion that such attachment is love. Such attachment leads to infatuation, lust, the need to gratify the senses, and greed.

People get caught up in conditional behavior that causes jealousy, possessiveness, suspicion, and doubts. Such a corrupt form of love is limited to the physical plane. The underlying belief here is that we *are* our physical bodies.

Many have realized that appearances are transient. They come and go. They realize the importance of seeing through superficial aspects and establishing a sound foundation for relationships based on lasting aspects like mental virtues and shared values. They experience love beyond the body. They appreciate the mental and intellectual traits of people to love them.

Appreciating and loving the inner beauty of people rather than their physical or material attributes is an important lesson for many people. This is a higher form of love where we love people for what they are "made of" instead of how they appear. The underlying belief in such love is that we are the mind and intellect.

Love that is limited to the physical or mental plane is still superficial. True love goes far deeper. The same consciousness lives and functions through each of us. On the outside, we may appear separate and different, but we all are diverse expressions of the underlying oneness. True love exists in the awareness of this oneness.

All of us have experienced this oneness at some point or the other. We experienced it as infants. As infants, we were literally swimming deep in the ocean of true love, as we knew no "other." Oneness alone prevailed. But now, we have risen to the surface of the ocean and believe in diversity. Our ultimate lesson is to re-discover and embrace our oneness.*

Most people do not consciously dive deeper to unravel this experience of true love. And yet, unknowingly, they get a glimpse of it when they feel unconditional love in any relationship. It could be a mother's love for her child, a lover's for their beloved, or the love between siblings.

When we catch a glimpse of true love in any relationship, we start longing for this glimpse again and again. We are drawn towards

---

* More on the Lesson of Oneness in Chapter 29

the person who served to give us this glimpse. When we feel unconditional love for someone, they give us a glimpse of our true Self. In the quest for love, we unknowingly seek our true Self, everywhere, in everyone.

Even the pleasure we seek in the world is actually the pursuit of the bliss of oneness. But due to the illusion of multiplicity, we wrongly believe that being in the company of a particular person brings us happiness. When this belief is reinforced, we struggle to preserve their company. We try to sustain their presence in our life forever.

This attempt to cling to people makes us feel insecure. This insecurity is at the root of many injured memories. And this attempt to cling to and possess the person in a relationship ends up ruining it.

Love begins to evaporate when these feelings of insecurity and possessiveness take over. Doubts prevail, leading to disillusionment. Insecurity and disillusionment are at the root of the most hurtful memories.

These memories and associated emotions can be healed by deeply understanding this topic and contemplating our emotions and inclinations.

3. Deal with the Source, not the channels

When we receive anything, we wrongly assume the channel through which we've received it as the source. We start expecting to receive further from the same channel and feel disheartened if the channel doesn't deliver the goods.

For example, someone's brother used to help him earlier but has stopped helping him. He says, "My brother has let me down." If the father does not assign a share of his property to his son, the son starts hating him. This is because people assume their relatives to be the givers, the source.

Most of us are habituated to expecting from the channels around us. When we need water, we draw it from the tap. Does the tap have any capacity for giving? The tap is just a channel for the water reservoir. There are many taps (channels) through which water is received, but they all come from the same water reservoir (the Source). When we insist that we want water only from a particular tap, we invite sorrow into our lives.

If you seek water directly from the reservoir, you will get more than you could ever ask for. You give up your limited perspective of expecting from a particular tap. You realize that there are many other channels through which the Source can give. Everything is abundant in the Source. It is common sense to expect from the Source rather than the channels.

With this clarity, you will begin to deal with the Source (God, Consciousness, the Self) alone in daily life. You will stop dealing with individuals and begin to see the Source in them. You honor the Source that works through them. You give to the Source and receive from the Source through all your dealings in the world.

You stop expecting love from individuals because you are convinced that whatever has to come, will come from the Source through some channel or the other. This is a powerful paradigm shift that gives true freedom. We stop relying on people to feel happy and loved.

4. Overcome hatred by choosing love

Where does hate come from? It comes from our deep fears. Where there is no fear, there can be no hatred. One who experiences hatred is intrinsically fearful. He feels helpless, rejected, disregarded, worthless, and like a victim.

When our fears overwhelm us, we feel the urge to direct the hatred outward. We mistakenly assume that doing so will make us feel empowered, and our fears will subside. But it only intensifies. So, we keep repeating this and get caught in the vicious cycle of hatred.

The only way to change this is to choose love.

Generally, people feel they can express love only when they experience the "right" feeling. They think, "I never feel like talking to this person nicely. So, I won't unless I 'feel' like it."

Think about it. Does a student say, "I won't study until I 'feel' like it?" Those who fall into this trap, fail their exams. Sincere students make up their mind, "I may not feel like studying, but I have a choice. I want to achieve my goals, so I'll study even when I don't feel like it."

Similarly, even if we don't "feel" love, we can indeed "choose" love because that's the lesson we are here to master. If we keep waiting for the feeling to arise, we will never be able to express love. We are making choices every moment of our life. So, choose love over hatred in all circumstances.

5. Love every aspect of the world

Every aspect of the world is an expression of the divine will. Out of ignorance, we prefer a part of this world and refuse to accept the other. Out of fear, we do not embrace the world in its entirety. We judge or hate the world for its imperfections. By judging or hating, we create more of it. All the imperfections we perceive are a shadow cast by our refusal to lovingly accept whatever is.

True love is always from the Self for the Self. It is not based on external conditions or the notion of separate individuals. If people appear good to us due to our attachment to them or at fault due to our aversion to them, then we are living in an illusion. Hence, we need to develop the eye of wisdom to see the oneness inherent in the diversity of life.

23

The Lesson of Courage

To understand the lesson of courage, we must first understand what fear is. At the deepest level of all our fears lies the fear of death. The fear of death is the fear that we won't exist.

Fear is useful to the extent of precaution. It is essential to safeguard ourselves from dangers that threaten our physical and emotional well-being. Fear also deters us from being rash and reckless in our choices and habits. But beyond that, it doesn't serve any purpose. Being prudent and cautious is one thing and being frightened is another.

In human life, the role of fear goes beyond the urge to survive and manifests as the fear of losing our identity. We all have unique identities that we are attached to. They are our name, family, group, community, physical appearance, background, likes, dislikes, etc. We define our existence based on such an identity that we have unconsciously assumed as "I." And then we fear that it might get lost or dented.

We try to identify with and cling to whatever follows "I am…"– I am a man, I am a woman, I am a mother, I am smart, I am sad, I am an artist. We get lost in the constant chatter of thoughts and emotional upheavals.

However, the truth is that we are none of these; we are the conscious presence, the Self. The feeling of "I am" is constant. Everything that follows "I am" keeps changing. They are our false identities. We fear losing them.

We do not just keep our identity limited to our body-mind. We get attached to our near-and-dear ones, thus investing in an identity based on being with them. Therefore, we fear the loss of our loved ones.

Some of us may not bother about the death of our body-mind as much as the death of our loved ones. Sometimes, the thought of the eventual death of our family member also haunts us. This fear is essentially the fear of our death; it's just that it appears different. It occurs because we have defined our existence in terms of their being alive with us. So, again, it is the fear of death of our identity.

Ironically, we fear separation from others because separateness is at the root of our assumed identity. We have moved away from oneness. Where there is oneness, there can be no fear.

All our injured memories, and past traumatic experiences, have always belonged to some false identity – never really to who-we-truly-are. Therefore, it wouldn't be wrong to say that every karmic scar, every injured memory, has a fear of death at its core. All negative emotions are based on fear. And our fears are based on ignorance of our true nature.

The fallacy of fear

Isn't it strange that we tend to avoid the feeling of fear even though we are familiar with it? We already know fear very well through our subjective experience. But we withdraw from it because we have never looked at it objectively for what it truly is.

Instead of looking at fear for what it is, we start perceiving people or situations through the lens of fear. It distorts our view of the world, due to which people or situations appear menacing to us. To understand fear objectively, we need to see it clearly from a distance. Then, we will see fear as an insignificant thing that we imagined to be real and substantial.

We feel threatened by our fears. The threat does not lie outside but in the imaginary story we have attached to our fears. Fear is a misuse of our imagination. The feeling of fear can be very intense, and yet it can be totally baseless. Given this, how much can we trust our fears?

At the subconscious level, we go by the intensity of the feeling of fear. The more intense the feeling, the more we react without a conscious choice. The urge to react to fear has been programmed through our DNA and the injured memories planted in us.

Generally, we react to fear in three ways: fight, flee, or freeze. We may muster courage and fight the source of the perceived danger, feel terrified and flee, or become immobilized and freeze. But there is also a fourth way… and that is courage!

Understanding courage

Courage is not the same as fearlessness. Fearlessness is the absence of fear, while courage involves taking action despite feeling fear.

Infants are often fearless as they are ignorant of the dangers around them. For example, if they see a lizard, they may fearlessly chase it as they have no prior conditioning. At the same time, an adult may scream and run away at its sight if they are conditioned to be afraid of lizards from their childhood. Courage is about consciously facing our fears and taking action, despite feeling terrified within.

People often rent ski gear like boots, poles, and bindings to practice skiing when visiting a ski resort. Likewise, whenever we encounter situations that trigger our fears, we can regard them as the gear we have hired to practice courage. Whenever we meet people or face situations that scare us, treat them as the practice ground nature has provided to hone our courage.

Practicing courage

Courage can be learned only through practice. The best way to achieve fearlessness is by repeatedly going through the experience of what we fear. Courage is the way to become fearless. Practicing courage consists of four steps:

1. Face the fear

Look at it in the eye, and it evaporates! For this, we must decide and overcome our initial discomfort. Whatever you are afraid of, approach it with an air of curiosity as if it were your first encounter.

If you are afraid of speaking in front of people, try and deliberately say a few words in a limited group to begin with. Observe the overriding feeling that is triggered and brush it aside. As you gain confidence, you can gradually experiment with a larger audience. If you are afraid to confront someone, find some pretext to go and break the ice.

2. Desensitize yourself through repetition

Due to repeated contact and friction with the ground, the soles of our feet become tough and less sensitive than the rest of the skin. The same principle can be applied to overcome our fears.

Initially, courage overcomes the intensity of fear. With repetition, we develop confidence and competence. We do what we fear so often that we become insensitive to it. Slowly the fear fades away.

Whatever we fear, be it open space, water, the stage, darkness, heights, or people, we must face it repeatedly until the associated fear becomes a thing of the past.

3. Learn to laugh at your fears

We all can laugh in comfortable situations. It takes courage and wisdom to laugh in the face of adversity. Learning to laugh at our own fears is more helpful than laughing at the fears and mistakes of others. Laughing can remove the associated feeling of fear and make us feel comfortable with the object of our fear.

4. Rationalize your fears

The fears we experience in most situations are baseless. They exist due to our injured memories that surface with resonating external circumstances. They can be overcome using common sense and rational thinking.

For example, a man goes for an interview. He is mortally terrified. He can overcome his fear by rationalizing it. He should ask himself, "Am I going to beg for something there? Will they beat me up if I don't perform well?"

He will find that he is responding to their job advertisement. If he doesn't perform, they will reject him. So, when he considers the worst that can happen, he will be free from fear. Instead, he will look at the positive side of gaining a useful experience of attending an interview.

In another example, you are afraid of cockroaches. You can ask yourself, "How can this little creature harm me? Can it bite me or injure me? Can't I deal with it easily? Who should fear whom? Should I fear the cockroach, or should the cockroach fear me?"

In this way, with rational thinking, we can overcome most of our fears and phobias.

Freedom from the ultimate fear

The ultimate fear at the root of every other fear is the fear of death. It is the fear of losing our identity.

Death never occurs. Our true Self is eternal. It is important not only to know this but also be convinced about this. Since people lack this conviction, they live in fear, always feeling incomplete and insufficient.

The remedy is to become familiar with our true nature. When we consistently contemplate and meditate, we transcend the realm of our emotions, thoughts, and sensations and directly experience the pure consciousness that we truly are.

The more we dip into the experience of pure consciousness, the more we gain conviction about our true nature, which is unshakable, untouched, and eternal.

24

The Lesson of Persistence

Persistence is essential to achieve anything worthwhile. It is the spirit of relentlessly persevering towards our chosen goal despite all odds.

History is replete with examples where people had no access to conveniences, facilities, or luxuries. They suffered setbacks. And yet they achieved their goals.

What is holding us back from achieving success? It is neither the setbacks nor the failures but the lack of persistence. We give up persisting for trivial reasons, even when it is possible to move on.

The hurdles of distraction and waywardness

It takes an uncompromising dedication and a single-pointed focus to accomplish any significant project. Today, we are facing an information overload, which makes it challenging to stay focused and work sincerely.

An increasing number of people suffer from an attention deficit. They have short attention spans and get easily distracted from work or study. They find it difficult to stick to tasks that are tedious or time-consuming. They feel the urge to switch from one task to another, like switching channels on TV.

We lack persistence because the mind rebels when tied to a given activity for an extended period. The mind becomes wayward and seeks distractions to kill the boredom that sets in. Most people suffer from boredom, which is turning into severe disease. The same instinct fuels wanderlust, making it difficult for people to stay in one place for long.

Link to traumatic memories

The root cause of lack of persistence is the discomfort felt while dwelling on a single thought stream or an activity stream. When the mind is constrained to one place, it experiences fear of death. This could also possibly be due to injured memories of being subjected to bonded labor without respite – a rampant practice in ancient and medieval times. The memory of the longing for freedom manifests today in the form of distractions and waywardness.

Another possible scenario that affects persistence is the fear of death upon completion of an endeavor. Such memories may stem from instances where people were subjected to hard labor, at the end of which they were blinded, muted, or executed. Imagine how someone would feel knowing that they will be put to death when their ongoing activity ends. They would never want the activity to finish in their vain attempt to ensure the continuity of their life.

These impulses run so deep at the subconscious level that they are not immediately perceptible at the conscious level.

But the lack of persistence need not always be linked to traumatic memories. It can just be the inability of an untrained mind to handle the overwhelming influx of entertainment and information. Indiscriminate indulgence of the mind inhibits persistence.

Challenges contributing to this lesson

Let us look at the possible challenges that indicate our lack of persistence.

- Inability to define precisely what is to be done.
- Tendency to work unplanned and haphazardly.
- Procrastination of tasks for no rational reason.
- Lack of interest in doing what matters.
- Finding excuses for not making progress.
- Tendency to blame others for our shortcomings.
- Branding adverse circumstances as showstoppers without a second thought.
- Fear of being criticized or ridiculed for failure.

If you notice any of the above signs frequently appearing in your daily life, you should consider persistence as a key lesson.

Ways to develop persistence

Many of us leave our tasks unfinished when faced with obstacles. We need to face obstacles with courage and willpower.

The first step in any endeavor is to develop clarity of purpose. We need to define our goal in measurable terms and why we want to achieve it. The clarity of our goal helps us persevere towards it.

Confusion is a major reason for our inability to persevere towards a chosen goal. When we are unclear about what to do, we procrastinate.

Instead, we should work towards gaining clarity and organizing ourselves without delay.

The converse is also true. We often wait for everything to be clear before starting work. We feel uncomfortable when things are ambiguous. At such times, we can still progress amidst the clouds of ambiguity. Clarity begins to emerge as we take a few steps forward. Torchlight in the dark only needs to illuminate the next few steps, provided we know the direction. When we start walking, the further steps are automatically illuminated.

Whenever the mind gives up in the face of showstoppers and says, "I can't do this," we should reframe this sentence as a question, "How can I do this?" This opens the mind to possibilities. We can tell the mind, "There are at least ten good ways to proceed from here. I only need to find one of them!" When we experience lethargy, confusion, or the urge to deviate, use the line "Do it, no matter what" as a mantra to accomplish work.

Persevering towards your goal

People experience dilemmas when they do not have a clear goal in life. They feel lost when there is no clarity about their life's purpose. These dilemmas undermine their resolve and persistence.

When one lacks clarity of purpose, his life is like a horse without reins, running helter-skelter. He is unable to direct his mental and physical energies. He wastes time on trivial matters, which delays his success. Hence, having a clear goal is of utmost priority.

When we set a clear goal, all our thoughts align in that direction. We experience a spurt in our willpower to achieve that goal.

But this is possible only when we always remember our goal. For this, it is necessary to write our goal. After writing the goal, read it, feel it, and live with it every day. We persist despite setbacks as we envision our goal before our eyes and live for it.

Consider two people, each with their own goals. The first person writes his goal everywhere—in his diary, on the mirror, on the whiteboard, as wallpapers on his phone, laptop, etc.

He talks about his goal to other people. They also guide and encourage him. In this way, his willpower increases, and his desire to achieve the goal intensifies.

The other person also sets a goal. But his goal is limited to his thoughts. After a few days, he forgets that he has set a goal for himself. He falls back to his old set patterns, and his will to achieve his goal drops.

Develop a resolute mind

The ultimate purpose of the lesson of persistence is to develop a steadfast mind that does not waver in the face of temptations or dire circumstances. A steadfast mind doesn't lose its direction in the short or long term.

The purpose of setbacks and temptations in our life is to test our inner strength and resoluteness. Our response in such situations indicates how resolute and unshakable we are. If we find it hard to resist temptations despite knowing the consequences, it highlights the urgency to strengthen our persistence muscle.

For example, when you sit for meditation, you may find that your mind is full of thoughts, and you may feel pain in some parts of your body. Resoluteness helps you to persist with the meditation practice despite all of this. If these distractions are holding you back from sitting in meditation, you need to work on being resolute.

One with strong resoluteness persists with his behavior even in the face of the hardest of adversities. He follows the principles and values he has set for himself, no matter what. Have you set your principles for life? If not, then decide them.

This is even more important for the youth to build a strong foundation of character. We see many youngsters wasting their precious years in the superficial and frivolous aspects of life, being caught up in the quicksand of social media and the Internet. The quality of persistence for higher values is essential for them to lead a truly fulfilling life. Only then can they accomplish the purpose of their Earth-life.

25

The Lesson of Empathy

All of us would have come across situations, where we shared our innermost sensitive feelings with the other person, and we felt that they didn't pay enough heed to us, even though they were apparently listening to us. We could see that their eyes were drifting to the surroundings. They were looking out of the window intermittently. They checked every notification on their phone. We felt they were disinterested in listening to us going by their body language.

Recall such a conversation and remember how you felt. Weren't you hurt? Even if they could repeat whatever you told them, you wouldn't believe that they heard you fully.

When we listen to others, our listening should not be limited to just hearing the words. We need to go beyond words and connect with the feelings that the words are emanating from. It comes with empathy.

Empathizing with people is about understanding where they are coming from, sensing what they deeply feel when they utter those words. If we are present with all our attention, sincerity, and sensitivity, we can connect with people at an experiential level. We can feel their emotions. This is nothing but "stepping into someone's shoes." Sometimes, just listening to people with such sincerity starts healing them. They start feeling better for no apparent reason.

Dr. Morgan Scott Peck, an American psychiatrist, describes his experiences in one of his books. In his patients' first few counseling sessions, he would only listen to their problems attentively and empathetically. Before he could even begin their treatment, 25% of them would already start feeling better. Thanks to his empathetic listening skill, even simply listening to someone attentively and empathetically acted as an effective therapy for them.

Generally, we seek to be understood first. While listening, many of us are eager to speak the moment we get an opportunity. We rarely listen with the pure intent of understanding.

Empathy is the ability to feel or see someone else's pain through their eyes. Being empathetic helps us to connect with others and understand them better. It is different from being sympathetic, which means feeling sorry or sad for people about their suffering.

Lack of empathy

Most of us operate from our heads rather than our hearts, due to which we cannot relate to others' feelings. Due to the hurtful scars from childhood or injured memories, we close our hearts to the outside world.

We feel unsafe to open up our feelings for fear of being hurt again. As a result, we neither express how we feel to others nor sense how they feel. We have trouble understanding our feelings when we step away from our heart and try to rationalize everything. In the process, unfortunately, we close our heart and shut ourselves to the beauty of life. We also find it difficult to relate to and live in harmony with people.

Challenges contributing to this lesson

We try to assess our ability to empathize by using our rational mind, which cannot sense the domain of the heart. Hence, it becomes difficult to determine whether we lack empathy. However, the following tell-tale signs can be of help. These signs indicate that we must develop empathy.

- We often tend to criticize people.
- We may not easily forgive others for their mistakes.
- We may feel that others don't understand us. (This mirror effect shows that perhaps we don't understand others' feelings either.)
- We keep blaming people who suffer.
- We find it difficult to relate to emotionally sensitive people.
- We are not usually concerned about the opinions of those around us.
- We get angry when we can't understand others.
- We do not realize when we inadvertently hurt others' feelings.
- We find it hard to imagine how we would feel in someone else's situation.
- We often stop listening to others if we can't agree with them.

Developing empathy

The first step towards developing empathy is to try and step into the other's shoes. Try to see things from their perspective without using our mental filters about how life should be perceived. This can provide a powerful perspective shift for us, especially if we are in conflict with the person we try to empathize with.

We need to set aside our prejudices and listen to others. Initially, we may find it difficult to put our biased lenses aside, but it helps to give others the benefit of the doubt and try to see how they are right.

This also invokes compassion to see others with forgiving eyes and bless them. When we start forgiving people and showering our blessings on them, we also start developing our sense of empathy.

26

Other SOUL Lessons – 1

Having elaborately discussed some of the key SOUL lessons, let us understand some more lessons that apply to many of us.

1. The lesson of resilience

Resilience is the ability to overcome failures or setbacks and bounce back. It is not merely based on the desire for things to get better. It stems from the conviction that life is meant to attain its highest potential.

When we lack resilience, we lose hope and allow doubt and despair to grow within us. We fall out of alignment with nature. Resilience is the triumph of hope over despair. It is the pivot that transforms seemingly bleak situations into opportunities for a better life.

Thomas Edison is the epitome of resilience. He is said to have failed about ten thousand times in his experiments to create the electric bulb. Without losing hope, he persevered and succeeded in bringing "light" into our lives! He considered his failures as steps in the learning process. In his words, he had never failed but succeeded in finding ten thousand ways that an electric bulb *won't* work.

Just as you exercise your body regularly to build your muscles, you also need to exercise regularly to build your resilience. Whenever you feel like giving up and say, "No, this is not possible," immediately reinforce the thought, "Just try it one more time and see."

A circus owner had pitched his circus tent on the outskirts of the city. A violent storm raged and blew away the tent just a day before the show. The owner was a veteran who had been through tough times. While the members of the troupe were running helter-skelter, worrying how they would put up the show, the trapeze artist saw the owner walking around with an enigmatic smile.

Reassured by his smile, the trapeze artist told others, "I have seen our boss smile. We don't need to worry. Let's talk to him." They approached him and asked what they should do next. Before instructing them on how to salvage the damaged tent, he cheered them up, "The tent may have blown away, but hold onto your happy hat, lest you lose that too… the show is far from over!"

So it is with our lives. When the storm of calamities comes, it may seem to ravage our life. But the least we can do is to hold on to our happy hat. H-A-T here also represents Hope, Awareness, and Trust. Hope can help us tide over the storms of life. Awareness enables us to steer clear of the injured memories that may weigh us down. By trusting our divine plan, we can move forward with courage.

2. The lesson of communication

Past life wounds related to communication can take a toll on our ability to express ourselves openly and confidently. Our inherited injured memories may cause us to feel low on self-morale. As a result, we may procrastinate communicating on important topics and thereby create complications in relationships.

The barriers we experience in communication can manifest as speech impediments like stammering, shyness, struggling to find the right words, repressing our emotions while speaking, and stage fright. We may shudder at the thought of being misunderstood and prefer to remain silent. The lesson here is to let go of our fears and inhibitions and develop the habit of clear and timely communication.

Many people with communication problems are over-sensitive to criticism. They go into their shell when criticized and avoid situations where they might face criticism. They need to learn to take criticism as constructive feedback and work on self-improvement playfully.

3. The lesson of collaboration

Those who have collaboration as their lesson are solitary workers. They prefer to work individually. They are most comfortable when asked to sit and work alone in a corner. They find it uncomfortable to work in interdependence with other people.

If collaboration is your lesson, life presents you with frequent opportunities for teamwork. You will be put into situations where you have to work with people, much against your will. You will be led through such experiences in relationships to remind you of this lesson of collaborating.

We are bound to have disagreements whenever we work in a team, at home, at our workplace, or elsewhere. When our perspectives do not align with those of other team members, we may feel the urge to leave the team.

A team is formed with a common vision, and it is natural to have different perspectives. This is the beauty of a team. It is okay to have

---

* Read the book *"Mastering the Art of Communication"* to understand the nuances of communication and develop effective communication skills.

people with diverse and conflicting perspectives. If the team has the same goal, we can still leverage conflicting ideas to create something new. We need to overcome our resistance to conflicts. Conflicts can be healthy and fruitful in a group.

The lesson is to get rid of our hang-ups about working with people. Working in teams allows us to develop many other qualities like patience, courage, confidence, communication, and acceptance.

4. The lesson of faith

Faith is the feeling of deep assurance in life. It is the force that brings our beliefs to fruition. When we completely trust something without a doubt, we exercise our faith.

Life without faith is like holding an umbrella over our heads. When faced with dire situations, we curse our luck and worry about why things happen to us. We pray for redemption, not knowing that blessings are already showering on us all the time. All we need to do is put away our umbrella! This is the umbrella of unnecessary fears and doubts that we unknowingly harbor at our subconscious level. These fears and doubts may come from our childhood conditioning, DNA, or the injured memories we have inherited. Faith helps us to drop this umbrella and enjoy the relentless flow of life.

Many people are fraught with doubts and find it difficult to trust people. They invariably echo the fear of betrayal that exists in their wounded memories. They doubt their family, friends, neighbors, and colleagues. They even doubt divine providence. They keep fluctuating from being believers in God to being atheists, based on the fulfillment of their wishes. Such people are also plagued by self-doubt.

---

* Read the book *"Awaken the Power of Faith"* authored by Sirshree, to understand how to develop the highest level of faith.

The lesson of faith is about moving from self-doubt to Self-belief (faith in the divine will of the Self). It is about releasing our faith in the miracle of life and letting go of our doubts and fears.

It will help to contemplate the following questions to assess your level of faith and foster it:

- What are the situations or incidents that shake my faith?
- How can I make my faith steadfast in such situations?
- How can I take my faith to such a height that it will never diminish?

These questions will help us know ourselves better and bring the current state of our faith to light. Once we know the current state, we can take steps to strengthen it.

5. The lesson of self-control

Self-control is an aspect of our life that is related to many other lessons. It is essential for developing patience and persistence.

People often lose control over their words in a hurry to react and end up hurting others. Once you abuse someone through your words, those words are irreversible. The resultant hurtful memories get etched in the mind of the recipients. They bear the burden of those injured memories. Moreover, you also incur karmic bondage. This is a sign of impulsiveness that can be overcome by developing awareness and patience.

Many of us are enslaved by our senses and indulge in sensory pleasures. Although our wise voice keeps guiding us, we often ignore it. Self-control is the underlying lesson for many of us.

We can practice delayed gratification, fasting of the senses, and mindfulness to nurture self-control.

---

* To develop self-control and boost willpower, read the book "*The Magic of Willpower*".

6. The lesson of forgiveness

We have discussed the duster of forgiveness as the most potent tool for erasing karmic scars and eradicating past life bondages.

However, forgiveness is also an important lesson for most of us. This is because the human ego is predisposed to get into a justifying mode and shirk off the responsibility of healing the past.

Holding grudges over the past only delays our freedom. Without realizing this, most people cling to resentful feelings and harbor hatred for those who have apparently wronged them. These feelings could also be fueled by injured memories planted within us. Therefore, forgiveness is a vital lesson for many of us – an essential theme of our Earth-syllabus.

In our everyday situations, even if others seem to be at fault, we easily forget that whatever comes our way is our own karmic payback that nature sends through them. If we grumble and complain, we only add more karmic scars, instead of healing them.

Hence, we must seek forgiveness from the bottom of our heart. It must be a genuine feeling that emanates from a clear understanding. When we seek forgiveness or forgive someone, we are only doing ourselves a favor, no one else. We are doing it to free ourselves from bondage.

The real benefits of this practice simply cannot be expressed in words. It can be felt only through direct experience. When you keep yourself free from karmic scars and feel the emptiness within, you feel sublime and blissful. You do not feel any stress or burden on your mind. When you experience the power of emptiness, you begin to love it and you will not allow even a single trace of karmic scars.

---

* Read the book, *"Seek Forgiveness & Be Free"* authored by Sirshree, to understand the nuances of forgiveness and effectively practice it in your life.

27

Other SOUL Lessons – 2

Let's understand some other lessons that can help bring harmony and smoothness to our everyday dealings with people.

1. Freedom from the urge to judge and criticize

We need not be judgmental in disagreeable situations. When we judge, we invariably reinforce our prejudices and ignore the other's point of view. Empathy helps us to be non-judgmental. When we give the other person the benefit of doubt, we learn much more about our blind spots.

We criticize people and also go to the extent of blaming God for whatever goes wrong. However, God never judges us for our biases and complaints. God lovingly gives us the freedom to choose how we wish to live. If we are bent on suffering, He allows us to suffer until we understand the futility. He gives us time to refine our perspectives and learn our lessons. We can take a cue from God and become non-judgmental.

Steps to overcome the urge to judge and criticize:
- Refrain from giving unsolicited advice.
- Stop jumping to conclusions without understanding the truth beyond the obvious.
- Focus on the positive in any incident and the virtues of people.
- Stay away from the company of critics.

2. Freedom from polarities

Be it people, objects, or events, we are conditioned to classify everything into pairs of opposites. This stems from a fundamental belief in duality. Hence, we label things as good or bad, superior or inferior, fair or unfair, great or mediocre, beautiful or ugly, etc.

Careful observation shows that polarities are an illusion. Everything is on a continuum that varies from the presence of something to its absence. For example, in an absolute sense, there is nothing like "hot" or "cold." Cold is just the absence of heat on the continuum of temperature. "Warm" is cooler than "hot." So, it is just a matter of perception. There is only one thing, not two opposites. Darkness is just the obstruction of light. Sorrow is the obstruction of happiness.

Catch yourself classifying things into pairs of opposites because it is the cause of all unrest and unhappiness. Freedom from polarities is a key milestone in the journey of attaining the experience of Oneness.

Steps toward freedom from polarities
- Whenever you catch the mind polarizing everyday happenings, use the mantra, "Happening is happening." This means whatever is happening is neither good nor bad,

neither wrong nor right. It is just happening! This helps to break the habit of polarizing.

- When you start witnessing every aspect of life without judgment, the habit of polarizing slowly fades away.
- Accept situations as they are instead of resisting them. Acceptance brings joy; resistance causes sorrow.

3. Freedom from the habit of comparison

Most people become disturbed and discontented due to their toxic habit of comparison. They go astray in life in a vain attempt to compare their physical attributes and material possessions with others.

We lose our originality due to the habit of comparison. Instead of nurturing our innate talent and developing our unique strengths, we try to copy others.

Parents and teachers compare children with their friends, neighbors, or siblings, thus planting the seed of this habit in their formative years. The child starts believing that he will be judged in comparison to others. He then begins to compare himself with others – a habit that dominates his Earth-life till the very end.

A doctor's friends are all in the engineering field, working with famous corporations, getting fat paychecks, and living lavishly. The doctor serves in a rural government hospital. He could have felt dejected by comparing his financial status and lifestyle with his friends. Instead, he pursues his inner calling and happily serves the patients. It is his lesson to attain contentment by serving selflessly. He will feel contented only by overcoming the habit of comparison.

When you see others progressing in their lives, instead of feeling disturbed, be happy for them. What is progress for you need not be progress for them. They are receiving everything according to their prayers and needs. You are already blessed with the power to achieve everything according to your divine plan. When you are convinced of this, you won't indulge in comparison.

Steps to freedom from comparison

- **Identify your originality**

    Instead of comparing yourself to others, contemplate your originality and uniqueness. "What do I really like? What do I truly enjoy? What am I an expert at? What are my SOUL lessons? What will give me everlasting contentment?"

- **Compete with yourself**

    If you wish to compare, then compare and compete with yourself. This comparison will propel you on the path of progress. If you're an athlete, try to break your records. If you're a student, get better at scoring more than your previous test. If you're a homemaker, compete with yourself for better pace and quality. Thus, you can turn the habit of comparison into a blessing.

4. Taking responsibility without stress

For many of us, our lesson is about fulfilling responsibility without being stressed. People often accept big responsibilities, but if something goes wrong, they lose their patience and vent their anger on others. They remain stressed till the work is completed.

Take higher responsibilities but learn to be a relaxed magnet. When we dwell in a state of peaceful assurance that the best will manifest according to our divine plan, we attract solutions and progress.

Many of us are sincere at work but avoid taking higher responsibilities because we cannot cope with the stress. The lesson here is to take responsibility by being relaxed.

Many people even inadvertently fall ill to escape responsibility. The moment they learn to accept responsibility willingly, their illness vanishes!

Steps for learning this lesson:

- Start small. Work on small manageable action plans.
- Keep affirming to yourself that taking responsibility is not a sign of burden but freedom. Welcome the responsibility by using positive words in your mind.
- Keep experimenting with new tasks and let go of your inhibitions.

5. Letting go of guilt and shame

The feeling of guilt or shame can be the result of injured memories planted within us. It can also be due to some so-called mistakes in our choices or actions from our formative years. Whatever the reason, if guilt is kept hidden, it will rot further and demoralize us. If it is shown the light of understanding, it will fade away.

The first way to throw some light on this is to talk to a well-wisher who can be trusted with our feelings. Not everyone deserves to know about what troubles us. People commit the mistake of sharing their stories with those who are undeserving and prone to misuse what they tell them. Hence, we should carefully disclose our feelings to someone worthy. Once this happens, the guilt or shame will come to the fore and fade away.

If there is no one with whom we can share our feelings, we can practice forgiveness. We should forgive ourselves for the guilt or shame we have held within. By being a detached witness to all the past impressions, we can release ourselves from our wrongdoings. By doing so, we can heal the painful memories of shame.

6. Freedom from anger

Many of us experience recurring situations that incite our anger and irritation. We justify our anger by blaming people, our environment, situations, and incidents.

When we are angry, we often harm others by our words or actions. But eventually, we realize that we have caused more harm to ourselves. Being angry is like punishing ourselves for others' mistakes. Anger doesn't solve anything. Instead, it can spoil everything.

Whenever we feel angry, we should step back and ask ourselves whether the matter deserves a response. Where there is anger, there is always pain underneath. Anger is a mask that we wear to conceal the pain and fear of our injured memories.

Deeply contemplate your life. Recall those moments when you were steamed up. What do you find? You will realize that there is something within you that makes you so anxious and irritated. Look deeper. You will begin to sense the suppressed stress of unfulfilled desires. Look still deeper. Why are you so attached to your desires? You will find some strongly held beliefs at the base of every desire.

Steps for freedom from anger

- Contemplate your anger: What is the real need for my anger? How can I achieve what I want without getting angry? Which hidden desire is causing this irritation?

- Creatively channel your anger. Many of us don't know the right way to express our feelings. We use anger to let out what we have suppressed. We can learn to creatively channel the energy of anger by using it for a constructive purpose.

- As soon as anger arises, focus your attention on the clock. Start counting. Observe how long the anger stays in your body. Make up your mind to reduce this timespan next time.

28

Other SOUL Lessons – 3

Let's continue understanding some more lessons that can help us progress on our inward journey to self-mastery.

1. The lesson of decision making

For may of us, decision-making is a mechanical process. Many of our decisions are influenced by our past choices. We avoid making decisions out of fear of failure or an undesirable outcome. We are afraid of taking responsibility for the consequences. Avoiding such situations does not bode well for making better choices in the future.

Not deciding is also a decision that brings its consequences. We can't avoid making decisions. Whether we postpone or avoid making decisions, we already decide one way or the other. The art of decision-making can be learned only by making decisions.

Our injured memories could be instilled with the fear of making decisions that caused harm or even death. Our childhood conditioning may also affect our ability to decide independently.

When we are indecisive, we gradually lose the ability to step out of our comfort zone and face life's challenges. Hence, we should start by making small decisions to boost our confidence. We will overcome our fears and learn to make major decisions in the process.

If decision-making is our lesson, nature presents us with challenges in the form of people who leave us alone in difficult times or criticize our choices. Don't lose heart. Seek advice from others but stop being compelled to follow them. With this comes the responsibility for our choices. Our choices may go wrong, but if we learn from the outcomes, we progress.

Decisions arising from higher awareness are right, although they may superficially seem wrong. Conversely, decisions arising from the mental noise of our ego are bound to go wrong, even though they may seem perfect on the surface.

Though our decisions may seem right to others, we must ask ourselves what our feelings and intentions are. If we act with lowered awareness, it is bound to backfire in the future. Those, who do not understand this, decide impulsively under the influence of their negative feelings. Their decisions are often driven by the need to avoid the uncomfortable feeling of insecurity or to please others. Hence, our decisions ought to be taken from a higher awareness.

2. The lesson of creative expression

Man is made in the image of God. Human life is a masterpiece created by God, which in turn is designed to create more masterpieces!

---

* To understand more about the nuances of effective decision making, read the book, *"Mastering the Art of Decision Making"* authored by Sirshree.

Creativity is one of the fundamental qualities that we are here to express. Nature imposes external constraints and inner inhibitions to hone our creative expression.

Creativity involves a new way of perceiving and expressing life. Creative expression emanates from the heart. However, due to the conditioning from our upbringing and injured memories, we drift away from the heart and end up living in the head. We fall out of alignment with the creative way of the heart and lead a reactive way of life, comparing and imitating the world.

Creativity thrives when we feel secure and confident. We feel open to the risks of making mistakes and challenging the status quo. We dare to be considered strange for straying from conventional ways. But for those whose lesson is creative expression, our past conditioning could be inflicted with self-doubt or the fear of rejection and ridicule.

Creative expression requires focus and discipline. Our creative energy can break out of old ways and innovate when directed appropriately. However, if we don't channel it constructively, it expresses itself in destructive ways. Hence, those who want to hone their creative expression must also develop their ability to choose wisely by listening to their intuition.

Many of us choose occupations based on the advice of others, under the influence of our financial conditions, or by following the herd instinct. We give up on what we love to do and settle for a career that either pays more or pleases the people who are important in our life.

The lesson of creative expression is learned by by letting go of our inhibitions and allowing our innate drive and talent to express. Like the decision-making lesson, this lesson can be furthered by experimenting in small ways, to begin with, and gradually taking on more creative challenges.

3. The lesson of abundance

There is an abundance of everything for everyone. It is the law of nature. Our limited thinking has caused us to draw boundaries and limit the flow of abundance.

For those of us who are miserly, it is not just limited to spending money but is expressed in many facets of our life. The tendency of miserliness can also manifest when it comes to giving love, attention, time, or effort. We also tend to be miserly with our words while appreciating others' virtues.

Miserliness stems from the fear of scarcity. This fear has plagued the human psyche since ancient times when resources were scarce, and survival was a challenge. We have inherited this fear through our DNA, injured memories, and upbringing. We have carried forward the fear of scarcity and the tendency of miserliness without questioning its present relevance.

Miserliness is also due to the belief that we lose what we give. This leads to the habit of amassing and hoarding things. We also unknowingly hoard toxic memories that burden and hinder us.

It is the law of nature that whatever we give, gets multiplied and returns to us manifold. If we give love, it returns to us multiplied. If we give attention, we get back more of it.

According to the divine plan, everything flows freely in everyone's life, be it love, time, happiness, prosperity, health, peace, or harmony in relationships. We can be ever connected to this flow unless it gets blocked due to our limiting beliefs.

To break the tendency of miserliness, we can start by setting aside a fixed amount of money to be donated to charitable causes. Donate selflessly without expecting anything in return.

---

* Read the book, *"The Source - Power of Happy Thoughts"* authored by Sirshree, to understand the Law of Abundance.

Start practicing by giving small things. Give a little time to someone, express gratitude, praise someone heartily, or buy books for a needy student, and see how it feels! The joy of giving can be known only by practicing it. Once you get a taste of it, you will love to give more and more. You will thus open yourself to the flow of abundance in your life.

4. Letting go of past grudges

Some people fall into the habit of amassing throughout their lives. They hoard not only material things but emotions and memories too, particularly painful ones. The lesson for them is to let go of everything that they cling to.

Some people feel hurt about very trivial things. They cannot take a single word spoken against them. If someone abuses or mocks at them, they feel deeply hurt. They hold it within for long, perhaps many years. They just can't let go easily. Every minor incident from childhood onward remains imprinted in their memory and affects their behavior. Their responses arise directly from their memories. They keep dragging the burden of bitterness throughout their life.

If you have such a habit, you need to contemplate: What memories are you clinging to that no longer serve you? Do you still hold grudges against a childhood neighbor or teacher for scolding or mocking you? Do the taunts of your friends or colleagues haunt you? Do the memories of some heart-wrenching experiences still disturb you? If so, you need to let go of them and seek forgiveness for having held onto such bitter memories for so long.

It helps to ask yourself, "What do I gain from the habit of hoarding memories of the past? Is there any benefit besides the suffering, pain, discomfort, and burden? Do I want to carry this burden for the rest of my Earth-life?" Questioning yourself this way convinces your mind to dispose of the trash of poor memories.

5. The lesson of receiving

We have seen that many people are afraid to give for fear of scarcity. But there are also people who do not like to accept help from others. They feel inferior to receive help. Such people have a subtle ego that says, "I only want to give, not receive." They find it disrespectful to receive anything from anyone. They believe that giving will glorify their self-image. Hence, they remain bereft of the joy of receiving.

To achieve higher goals of life, we need the help of many people. A person cannot attain the zenith of success all by himself. If you feel uncomfortable seeking or receiving help from others, or if you have a strong feeling that you can manage it all alone without help from anyone, then "receiving" is your lesson. Rise above the idea of superiority and inferiority. All help is Self-help.

The other subtler aspect of receiving is about allowing others to experience the joy of giving. When we stand stubbornly, denying any help, even when people happily offer us help, we deny them the joy of giving. So, even if we feel we can manage everything independently, we can be generous by allowing others to give to us!

6. Openness for the unknown

Many of us feel nervous about meeting new people, visiting new places, or marrying someone we hardly know. The fear of unknown makes us feel insecure.

If we insist that we must know everything upfront about something, someone, or some place before experiencing it, then "being open for the unknown" is our lesson.

Consider each day as a page in the book of life. Only after reading the first page will the next page unfold. Our whole life does not manifest suddenly. It unfolds one scene after another. Thus, every scene is a preparation for the next scene. No one knows what will happen in the next scene. What turn the situation takes is unknown. As the unknown is hidden, it gives a feeling of discomfort.

The results of our school or university exams are unknown. The reports of our medical diagnostic tests are unknown. Before marriage, our life partner may be unknown. How our business will perform is unknown. The future performance of the stock market is unknown. We remain anxious amid all these unknown aspects of life.

While these are some unknown external factors of our life, we are negligent about our inner truth, which is a profound mystery. When we begin to practice meditation, we unravel the hidden dark corners of our mind, which can often be an unpleasant experience. Many of us avoid practicing meditation to escape this discomfort. No one else can shed light on our inner truth, nor can we search for it on the Internet! It is only by enduring these inner experiences and facing the play of our ego that we can learn about our inner truth.

7. The lesson of allowing

Many people assert authority over their relationships. They try to control the lives of others. They impose their expectations of how others should behave. If people don't toe their line, they try to forcefully mend them. They are stressed by their sense of ownership. Those who live with them find it difficult to cope with them and live freely.

Their lesson is to let go of their need for control and allow others to express themselves. Their new motto should be, *"Live and let live."*

Every human being is a unique and beautiful creation of God. Everyone's needs and likes are different. We should learn to admire and wonder at the diversity of God's creation. Respect others' feelings and allow them to live as they want. When we allow people to express themselves, we will begin to experience harmony in our relationships. "Allow" means "I Love!"

When we control others, we resist the way people and things are. We, in turn, lose our peace and make life miserable for ourselves and others. We should develop an attitude of acceptance. Accept everything and everyone as they are. This will dissolve our resistance. Only then can we experience the beauty of relationships.

8. Freedom from the victim mindset

"I have no control over situations. Other people are always taking advantage of my situation. No matter what I try to do, all bad things keep happening to me." Such thoughts are a strong indication of a victim mindset. If we blame others for the incidents or situations in our life, we may be struggling with a victim mindset.

Such a mindset can be the result of past life trauma – either from injured memories or upbringing. At its core, such a mentality is primarily rooted in suffering and distress. Without ways to cope with the situations or incidents, bitter experiences lead to a strong negative mindset of blame and helplessness.

Due to the victim mindset, we firmly believe that life keeps happening to us, and there is nothing we can do about it. Even though there could be ways to overcome the circumstances of our life, we shun our responsibility and blame others or our destiny.

Many people cling to the idea of being a victim because they enjoy the sympathy and attention others shower on them.

We can confront the victim mindset and overcome it by learning about the laws of thought. We are the architects of our life. We can either choose to remain victims and suffer or create a powerful life and thrive.

---

*Read the book *"The Source - Power of Happy Thoughts"* authored by Sirshree to overcome a victim mindset and take charge of your life.

Whenever we feel low with the underlying belief, "I am helpless, I am a victim," reframe it with, "If I can choose to be sad, I can surely choose to be happy. I choose to celebrate life!"

The situations that make us feel victimized are waiting for us to take responsibility and heal them. It helps to remember that the Self has chosen us to heal our injured memories. We alone can resolve our incomplete memories for which the Self has appointed us! This new revelation can erase our past beliefs of victimhood.

9. The lesson of gratitude

When we are caught up in the whirlwind of negative feelings during testing times, we resort to blaming and cursing people, situations, and our fate. We react in ways that aggravate our karmic bondages. At such times, it helps to shift our mindset by invoking the power of gratitude.

We experience divine grace in every moment of our life. However, we take the most invaluable aspects of life for granted. Life itself is precious beyond measure. Being alive itself is the supreme grace. But most of us go through life without recognizing the value of being alive. Ask someone gasping for breath on his deathbed the value of breath and the value of life.

The oxygen we breathe, the water we drink; the daylight that illumines our activities; our parents and others who have supported us since childhood; the language we are taught by our parents and teachers, and them by their forefathers; our family who supports us in all possible ways; our friends who make it possible for us to share and grow; the hard work of the farmers; the technological advancements made possible by the relentless toil of scientists and engineers; the roads and vehicles enabling our travel; the founders and management of the organizations we work for, making it possible for us to express our skills and earn our livelihood; the power supply and distribution services that enable all our activities; the civic facilities that make organized community life possible in our cities, towns, and villages; the government that ensures continuity of life through its various departments; the anatomy and physiology of our body that work beautifully in ways beyond our imagination; the cosmic orchestra that works to perfection, making Earth – our home – a habitable place; the opportunity to learn our lessons; the grace of being considered worthy of healing the past... the list is endless.

As we heal our injured memories, we become more open to all of this, and more attuned to Oneness, our true nature.

So, it helps to contemplate everything we have. Then the truth shines forth that without the support of others, nothing is possible in our life. Whatever comes to us is a blessing.

When we dwell in the feeling of gratitude, our life attains new heights. The feeling of gratitude infuses positive vibes around us. If we are grateful for "everything in life" we automatically overcome doubts, worries, and feelings of lack. We automatically and constantly focus on the best; therefore, we receive the best.

When we learn the lesson of gratitude, the haze of ignorance and negativity vanishes, and we start working on the real purpose of life.

29

The Final Lesson

The final lesson of life that fulfills our SOUL purpose is to work towards being established in the expererience of the Self. If one does everything else without learning this lesson, they can never experience true contentment.

Contemplate the lives of Self-realized souls like Saint Kabir, Saint Meera, Saint Rumi, Saint Rabia, or Saint Dnyaneshwar. All of them had a commonality since their childhood. They kept getting profound questions, such as, "Who am I? What is the purpose of this existence? If the world is transient and short-lived, then what lives on? What is eternal?" These questions intensified their quest for the truth of life. They followed the guidance of their intuition and devoted their lives to seeking the truth of life.

Even today, such questions occur to many of us, "What is the purpose of my life? If God exists, what is the way to connect with

God? Am I just this body that I see in the mirror, or something beyond it?"

These people start seeking the Truth. They embark on a journey inward with the guidance of the Guru. They listen to the Truth, meditate, contemplate, and study spiritual literature.

The experience of Oneness

The Divine play on Earth is known to its Creator alone! The Self has manifested as myriad beings to enjoy this divine play. The Self experiences itself through humankind. There is none other than the Self. The experience of the Self is that of Oneness with all that exists.

During Earth-life, we are constrained by the limited viewpoint of our body-mind. This creates an illusion of diversity and separateness, which is at the root of all injured memories. Ignorance of our true nature is the root cause of this.

As we have seen in Part 1 of the book, the same consciousness works through every being. Separateness is an illusion. The lesson of re-discovering our true nature is the journey of transcending separateness to experience oneness.

We first learn to delve inward to experience pure consciousness as our inner experience. We then discover that this experience is all-pervading, beyond the body-mind. It pervades the entire creation.

How can we experience oneness when we live a life of diversity, conditioned by our name, form, religion, profession, and financial status? Let us understand this.

A million labels may get attached to our identity, but the aliveness, the feeling of living presence is the same in all of us. This experience of presence adorns various personality masks and plays multiple roles. This aliveness is the common thread that runs through everything, witnessing itself as the oneness playing all kinds of characters.

The ego is the notion of having a separate individual existence. Most of us are bound by a strong memory of individuality that shrouds the experience of oneness. Oneness is always the underlying reality. Separateness is merely an illusion projected over this oneness due to ignorance.

The melting of our ego is a prerequisite for experiencing oneness. The fire of wisdom should be kept burning with the oil of devotion to melt the ego. We need to develop detachment from our identification with the body-mind. The illusion of "I, Me, Mine, You, Your, They, Their, Them" shrouds the experience of our true nature. This illusion should be clearly seen and transcended in every situation.

With the relentless practice of remembering our true nature, we develop the conviction that we are beyond our personalities, body, mind, intellect, and all the associated beliefs and memories.

Initiators of the quest for truth

The inner calling to learn this lesson may occur at any age. Awakening may happen at any time. Some get inner inspiration after listening to just a single discourse of the truth. It touches their inner being and paves the way to liberation.

Some may receive this inner calling upon witnessing the death of their dear ones. This single incident completely steers their life towards the ultimate purpose.

For some of us, this book may come as a wake-up call to contemplate our life and discover the truth, leading to liberation.

Ways to learn the ultimate lesson

Following are some practices and perspectives that can help in the journey of Self-alignment.

1. The Supreme in Thee

Nurture the habit of witnessing God in everyone and everything. Whenever you feel hurt or let down while dealing with people, remind yourself, "*The Almighty in me, the Supreme in Thee!*" Use every opportunity to honor the divine presence within everybody, including your body. Start verbalizing this mantra. If this world is a divine creation, then all the virtues and vices are part of divinity. Meditate on the creator behind this grand illusion.

2. Self-encounter with awareness

Practice asking yourself over and over again, "Who am I now? Am I attached to the character?" For example, if your manager rebukes you and you feel insulted, ask yourself, "Exactly who was insulted? Am I this employee, or is it merely a role that I am playing? Who am I now?" If you feel hurt by the attitude of your children, ask yourself, "Who am I now? Am I attached to the character of a parent? Or am I the real 'I' beyond all these roles?"

These questions can awaken you to your true nature. They can deepen the experience of oneness. Asking questions helps you detach from the character, the role you are playing, and establishes you in oneness.

3. Don't stop with mere relief

If our SOUL purpose is to abide in Self-experience, we should be wary of the trap of material attractions. In the illusory world of attractions, success is defined in terms of our material wealth, fame, luxuries, comforts, and a sense of pleasure.

Very few are aware of the supreme success that comes with Self-experience. It is the ultimate purpose of all other forms of success.

---

* For an deep understanding of the journey to Self-realization and being established in Self-experience, read the book "*Journey to Enlightenment*" authored by Sirshree.

The feeling of relief is a mere milestone in our journey. Hence, we should not stop with mere relief or pleasure. We must keep progressing till we begin to gravitate towards the experience of the Self in every situation.

4. Consistent practice

The more a seeker of truth remains consistent in his practice of listening to the truth, meditating, and introspecting, the deeper he grasps the truth. Consistent practice is the key to supreme success.

30

Our Impersonal Mission

In 1952, scientists conducted an experiment on an island in Japan to study the behavior of a species of monkeys. They would provide an experimental group of monkeys with potatoes dropped in the sand. The monkeys liked eating potatoes but did not like the sand sticking around them.

One of the monkeys stumbled upon a solution. It washed the potatoes in a nearby stream. It demonstrated this to the other monkeys. They also started washing the potatoes in the stream before eating. This practice spread by observation until, say, ninety-nine monkeys learned to wash their potatoes before enjoying them.

The hundredth monkey that learned this practice caused a breakthrough that astounded the scientists. No sooner had it learned this practice than the scientists observed that suddenly, on the same day, all the monkeys on the island started following this practice. It was as if the collective learning of the skill in the first hundred monkeys sparked an automatic adoption of the same skill in the entire tribe of monkeys on the island.

And it didn't stop there! This learning of washing potatoes crossed the sea. Monkeys from other islands, hundreds of kilometers away, also started washing potatoes on the same day!

The scientists deduced that when a certain critical number achieves an awareness, this new awareness gets transmitted all over, even to remote locations. This came to be known as the Hundredth Monkey Phenomenon.

What this means is that new learning or behavior remains restricted to a limited number of people when only they practice it. But when the number of people aware of this behavior reaches a threshold, it gets transmitted to everyone else, regardless of whether they are in direct contact with the original group or separated across continents!

And this is not just limited to monkeys. It works for all living beings, of course including human beings, because the underlying consciousness serves as the medium for collective learning.

So, what does this mean for us? It means a lot!

When we work on our SOUL lessons to resolve our injured memories, we heal our life. But when more and more of us start working towards this purpose, we will eventually reach a threshold when the healing takes a quantum jump and pervades the entire humankind.

This also means that mastering our SOUL lessons is not our personal endeavor. We are rendering an impersonal service to elevate mass consciousness.

As we have understood in Part 1 of this book, the universal consciousness gets stained by the karmic scars held in the memory pool. These scars pollute the consciousness of the human biosphere. When we heal our memories, we contribute to the universal healing of consciousness.

Children play the game of building a house of cards by placing playing cards one on top of the other in a triangular formation. If you remove even a single card from the formation, the entire house of cards starts tumbling down.

The world's problems are like a cosmic house of cards, and we all are contributing our cards to it. This whole house of negativity can be razed to the ground just by removing our own card from it. We can remove our card by practicing forgiveness, letting go of our karmic impressions, and learning our SOUL lessons. We do our bit, and the gamut of problems can dissolve.

We need to approach our SOUL purpose as an impersonal service. As we've discussed in Chapter 6, the fingers inside the pot are at the service of the hand outside it. As we can now see, all help is Self-help. We *are* the duster, the cutter, the spectacles, and the torch that Consciousness uses to heal itself.

The lesson of impersonal service

Rendering impersonal service for universal healing and elevation of consciousness could be our SOUL lesson. This is the sole purpose for which many of us have been born on Earth.

Nature keeps creating opportunities for us to render impersonal service. Even if we ignore this mission and try to escape our inner calling, we will feel suffocated with everything else we do.

We may have every material thing that we need in life. Yet, we may feel discontented, as if something is missing. Nature keeps nudging us, reminding us of our mission. We may be frequently placed in situations where we are made to serve selflessly.

There could be some who have already learned the lesson of aligning with the Self. They only need to understand the divine design of life and lead a life of surrender to the divine will.

Our life is much like that of a caterpillar that sacrifices itself to go through the stage of the cocoon and then strives out of it. The struggle of the caterpillar to emerge from the cocoon strengthens its wings. Only then does the butterfly emerge and fly in all glory.

Similarly, we must dedicate ourselves to the impersonal mission of tiding through limitations in life to heal our share of injured memories and develop the strength to attain the pinnacle of human potential.

SOUL Lessons and Their Contributing Challenges

Sr. No.	SOUL lesson	Contributing challenges
1.	Patience	Restlessness, Loss of temper, Haste, Tendency to react impulsively and choose shortcuts, Face frequent delays
2.	Unconditional Love	Bitterness, Hatred, Habit of holding grudges, Mental loneliness, Feeling distanced from others, Feeling unloved
3.	Courage	Fear of losing identity, Fear of loss of loved ones, Lack of confidence, All imagined fears
4.	Persistence	Lack of clarity of the goal, Unplanned workstyle, Procrastination, Lack of interest, Blaming others for one's shortcomings, Branding situations as adverse without second thought, Fear of criticism or ridicule
5.	Empathy	Habit of criticizing people, Inability to forgive and relate to emotionally sensitive people, Unconcerned about others' opinions, Angry of inability to understand others, Tendency to hurt others unknowingly
6.	Resilience	Loss of hope, Feeling of despair, Lack of trust in Divine plan.

7.	Communication	Low self-morale, stammering, shyness, Inability to express openly and confidently, Inability to find the right words, Suppression of emotions while speaking, Stage fright
8.	Collaboration	Prefer to work individually, Difficulty working in teams, Frequent disagreements, Discomfort in conflicts.
9.	Faith	Plagued by doubts and fears, Lack of trust on people, Selfdoubt, Tendency to give up easily.
10.	Self-control	Indiscriminate indulgence in sensory pleasures, Impulsive with speech.
11.	Forgiveness	Self-righteousness, Tendency to justify one's actions, Holding grudges of the past, Clinging to resentful feelings.
12.	Overcoming the urge to judge and criticize	Habit of jumping to conclusions without looking beyond the obvious, Tendency to overlook others' perspectives, Habit of criticizing others.
13.	Freedom from polarities	Tendency to categorize things in opposites like good-bad, wrong-right.
14.	Freedom from the habit of comparison	Tendency to borrow others' values, Habit of copying others, Compare one's life, possessions, or attributes with that of others, Ignorance one's originality or uniqueness
15.	Responsibility without stress	Anger on others for unaccomplished tasks, Escapism from taking responsibility, Perceiving responsibility as a burden.

#		
16.	Letting go of guilt and shame	Self-blame, Feeling demoralized, Inability to express feelings openly
17.	Freedom from anger	Tendency to blame others, Blurting out words or acting in ways harming to self and others, Fear and irritation within.
18.	Decision making	Fear of failure and undesired outcomes, Fear of making mistakes and owning the consequences, Lack of confidence, Fear of others' criticism, Habit of deciding impulsively from lowered awareness or negative feelings.
19.	Creative expression	Ego-centered living, Inability to tune into the heart, Reactive way of life, Compare and imitate others, Selfdoubt, Fear of rejection and ridicule, Occupation based on others' advice or herd instinct.
20.	Abundance	Miserliness for money, love, attention, good words, time, Fear of scarcity, Belief that one loses what one gives, Habit of hoarding.
21.	Letting go of past grudges	Feeling hurt over trivial matters, abuses, mocks, Clinging on to hurt feeling for long.
22.	Receiving	Dislike receiving help from others, strong feeling that everything can be managed by oneself.
23.	Openness for the unknown	Feeling insecure about meeting new people, visiting new places, Insistence to know everything upfront, Anxiety in unpredictable situations.
24.	Allowing	Assert authority in relationships, Control others, Impose expectations on others, Lack respect for others' feelings.

25.	Freedom from the victim mindset	Hold others responsible for one's situation, Feeling of helplessness, Enjoy sympathy and attention from others.
26.	Gratitude	Blaming people and situations, Feeling doubtful, Lacking trust, Feeling of lack.
27.	Oneness	The ego-sense of separateness

◆ ◆ ◆

You can mail your opinion or feedback on this book to:
books.feedback@tejgyan.org

About Sirshree

Sirshree's spiritual quest, which began during his childhood, led him on a journey through various schools of philosophy and meditation practices. He studied a wide range of literature on mind science and spirituality. After a long period of deep contemplation on the truth of life, his quest culminated in attaining the ultimate truth.

Sirshree espouses, "All spiritual paths that lead to the truth begin differently but culminate at the same point – Understanding. This understanding is complete in itself. Listening to this understanding is enough to attain the Truth." Over the last two decades, he has dedicated his life to raising mass consciousness.

Sirshree has delivered more than 4000 discourses that throw light on this understanding. He has designed a system for wisdom, which makes it accessible to all. This system has inspired people from all walks of life to progress on their journey of the Truth. Thousands of seekers join in a virtual prayer for World Peace and Global Healing daily at 9:09 am and 9:09 pm.

About Tej Gyan Foundation

Tej Gyan Foundation is a non-profit organization founded on the teachings of Sirshree. The Foundation disseminates Tejgyan – the wisdom that guides one from self-development to Self-realization, leading towards Self-stabilization.

The Foundation's system for imparting wisdom has been assessed by international quality auditors and accredited with the ISO 9001:2015 certification. This wisdom has been presented in a simple, systematic, and practically applicable form that makes it accessible to people from all walks of life, regardless of religion, caste, social strata, country, or belief system.

The Foundation has centers in more than 400 cities and towns across India and other countries. The mission of Tej Gyan Foundation is to create a highly evolved society by leading seekers from negative to positive thoughts and further, from positive thoughts to Happy thoughts. A 'Happy thought' is the auspicious thought of being free from all thoughts, leading to the state of supreme bliss beyond thoughts.

If you seek such wisdom that leads you beyond mere knowledge, dissolves all problems, frees you from all limiting beliefs, reveals the true nature of divinity, and establishes you in the ultimate truth, then it is time to discover Tejgyan; it is time to rise above the mundane knowledge of words and experience Tejgyan!

The MahaAasmani Magic of Awakening Retreat

Self-development to Self-realization towards Self-stabilization

Do you wish to experience unconditional happiness that is not dependent on any reason? Happiness that is permanent and only increases with time? Do you wish to experience love, peace, self-belief, harmony in relationships, prosperity, and true contentment? Do you wish to progress in all facets of your life, viz. physical, mental, social, financial, and spiritual?

If you seek answers to these questions and are thirsty for the ultimate truth, then you are welcome to participate in the MahaAasmani Magic of Awakening retreat organized by Tej Gyan Foundation. This is the Foundation's flagship retreat based on the teachings of Sirshree.

The Purpose of this Retreat

The purpose of this retreat is that every human being should:

- Discover the answer to "Who am I" and "Why am I?" through direct experience and be established in ultimate bliss.
- Learn the art of living in the present, free from the burden of the past and the anxiety of the future.
- Acquire practical tools to help quieten the chattering mind and dissolve problems.
- Discover missing links in the practices of Meditation (*Dhyana*), Action (*Karma*), Wisdom (*Gyana*), and Devotion (*Bhakti*).

About Books by Sirshree

Sirshree's published work includes more than 150 book titles, some of which have been translated into more than 10 languages. His literature provides a profound reading on various topics of practical living and unravels the missing links in karma, wisdom, devotion, meditation, and consciousness.

His books have been published by leading publishing houses like Penguin, Hay House, Bloomsbury, Wisdom Tree, Jaico, etc. "The Source" book series, authored by Sirshree, has sold over 10 million copies. Various luminaries and celebrities like His Holiness the Dalai Lama, publishers Mr. Reid Tracy, Ms. Tami Simon and Yoga Master Dr. B. K. S. Iyengar have released Sirshree's books and lauded his work.

The Source
Attain Both, Inner Peace
and Worldly success

Awaken the Power of Faith
Discover the 7 Principles of the
Highest Power of the Universe

To order books authored by Sirshree, login to:
www.gethappythoughts.org
For further details, call: +91 9011013210

SELECT BOOKS AUTHORED BY SIRSHREE

  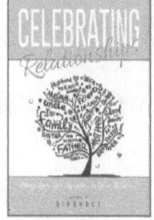 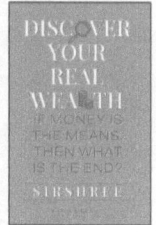

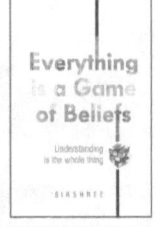   

To order these and other books authored by Sirshree
Visit **www.gethappythoughts.org**

Tej Gyan Foundation – Contact details

Registered Office:
Happy Thoughts Building, Vikrant Complex, Near Tapovan Mandir, Pimpri, Pune 411017, INDIA. Contact: +91 20-27411240, +91 20-27412576

MaNaN Ashram:
Survey No. 43, Sanas Nagar, Nandoshi Gaon, Kirkatwadi Phata, Off Sinhagad Road, Taluka Haveli, Pune district - 411024, INDIA. Contact: +91 992100 8060.

WORLD PEACE PRAYER

Divine Light of Love, Bliss, and Peace is Showering;

The Golden Light of Higher Consciousness is Rising;

All negativity on Earth is Dissolving;

Everyone is in Peace and Blissfully Shining;

O God, Gratitude for Everything!

Members of Tej Gyan Foundation have been offering this impersonal mass prayer for many years. Those who are happy can offer this prayer. Those feeling low or suffering from illness can receive healing with this prayer.

If you are feeling troubled or sick, please sit to receive the healing effect of this prayer. Visualize that the divine white healing light is being showered on earth through the prayers of thousands and is also reaching you, bringing you peace and good health. You can dwell in this feeling for some time and then offer your gratitude to those offering the prayer.

A Humble Appeal

More than a million peace lovers are praying for World Peace and Global Healing every morning and evening at 9:09. This prayer is also webcast on YouTube at 9:00 pm. Please participate in this noble endeavor.

www.ingramcontent.com/pod-product-compliance
Lightning Source LLC
LaVergne TN
LVHW041709070526
838199LV00045B/1269